Workplace Conflict Resolution Essentials

FOR
DUMMIES
A Wiley Brand

by Vivian Scott

FOR
DUMMIES
A Wiley Brand

Workplace Conflict Resolution Essentials For Dummies®

Published by
Wiley Publishing Australia Pty Ltd
42 McDougall Street
Milton, Qld 4064
www.dummies.com

Copyright © 2015 Wiley Publishing Australia Pty Ltd

Authorised adaptation of *Conflict Resolution at Work For Dummies* © 2010 John Wiley & Sons, Ltd. (9780470536438).

The moral rights of the author have been asserted.

National Library of Australia
Cataloguing-in-Publication data:

Author:	Scott, Vivian, author.
Title:	Workplace Conflict Resolution Essentials For Dummies / Vivian Scott.
ISBN:	9780730319450 (pbk.)
	9780730319504 (ebook)
Series:	For Dummies.
Notes:	Includes index.
Subjects:	Conflict management.
	Mediation and conciliation — industrial.
	Personnel management.
	Communication in personnel management.
	Work environment.
Dewey Number:	658.4053

Cover image: © iStock.com/timsa

Typeset by diacriTech, Chennai, India

Printed in Singapore by
C.O.S. Printers Pte Ltd

10 9 8 7 6 5 4 3 2 1

Contents at a Glance

Table of Contents

Introduction

. . . .

*E*very day in offices, retail stores, factories and any number of other workplaces, people are having conflicts with co-workers. It's normal, natural and nothing to fear. When handled properly, conflict can actually create positive changes and new opportunities in your organisation. Successfully making the shift in your perspective from seeing only the negative in disagreements to seeing the prospect for positive change is the first step to resolving difficulties.

To find positive outcomes in what on the surface looks like a negative situation, you have to become skilled at calming the infernos by helping employees through discussions that prove to them that they can solve their own issues. Become a coach for your team and colleagues — someone they can trust to bring the real and right issues to the table for effective problem solving.

If you can broaden your perspective to include the other person's point of view, you're sure to come out of the dispute with a better working relationship. Being at the centre of controversy is never a good idea for anyone, so decide to use the uneasy situation as an opportunity to improve systems, relationships, and your credibility.

In this book, I tell you what the most common causes of workplace conflict are and how to address them by using a proven mediation method and philosophy. And remember: Every story always has more than one side.

About This Book

This book is a tool intended to help managers (or anyone who has a job) work through conflict with peers, subordinates and even bosses. It's primarily aimed at those employees in organisations who find themselves negotiating difficulties without the benefit of having professional conflict resolution or mediation experience.

Although my focus is on how to facilitate conflict resolution, if you're the person experiencing conflict, this book outlines the kinds of structures that may be in place to support you, and what will be expected of you during each step of the process. Throughout the book, I also highlight the kinds of attitudes (such as good communication, getting to the underlying issues of the conflict and taking personal responsibility in finding a solution) that can help everyone avoid workplace conflict, no matter what level.

The chapters are chock-full of facilitation techniques and tools that come from successful conflict resolution experts, delivered in a way that's easy to understand and ready for you to apply right away.

To help make this book easier to navigate, I include the following conventions:

- ✔ I introduce new terms in italics and then define them.
- ✔ I use bold text to highlight key words in bulleted lists.

Foolish Assumptions

I'm assuming you have a job, paid or volunteer, and that you interact with people. I'm also assuming you have some sort of responsibility — be it keeping the line moving at the manufacturing plant or trying to keep your reputation intact as the star manager in the strongest department of an international corporation. And I'm thinking you're currently experiencing some trouble. You may be sick and tired of a conflict between two of your employees, you may be bickering with a colleague, or perhaps you're at a loss as to what to do about the problems between you and your boss. My final assumption? I'm guessing you want to do something about it.

Icons Used in This Book

Throughout the book you'll notice icons in the page margins to signal something I want you to pay particular attention to. Here are the icons I've used and what each represents.

If I know an easier way to do something or have an idea for creating a better working environment now and in the future, this icon tells you that.

I use this icon to flag some important information that you don't want to forget.

This icon alerts you to common blunders that you want to avoid.

Where to Go from Here

Workplace Conflict Resolution Essentials For Dummies is a book I hope you refer to again and again. You don't have to read it cover to cover to gain the insight you need to deal with conflict at work. You can flip to the chapter that best meets your needs today and come back to other sections as needed.

You may have a bookshelf full of management how-to tomes, but it's still a good idea to start with understanding what makes an employee tick and why she sees the world the way she does, so start with Chapter 2 to get right to the heart of the matter.

If you feel you have a pretty good handle on how emotions, values and group dynamics contribute to conflict, and you're ready to mediate a problem between two or more people, head straight to Chapter 6 and follow through to Chapter 10.

Finally, if you feel you may be in over your head and you'd like to find out more about how to enlist the help of an expert, check out Chapter 11 to see what your company may be able to do.

Although this book is designed so that you can start anywhere, don't feel obligated to jump around. If you're a traditionalist who likes to read every book from cover to cover, just turn the page!

Five Things You Can Control When in an Unresolved Conflict

- **Your plan for the future:** Consider what's important to you and follow a strategy for a period of time that feels comfortable. Knowing what you want your future to look like helps you look past the current situation and focus beyond temporary problems.

- **Your perspective:** Instead of staying wrapped up in a conflict, ask yourself whether you can find a learning opportunity somewhere in the situation. Or maybe if you purposefully and mindfully examine what's going on, you can honestly say, in the scope of things, the disagreements aren't really that important to you.

- **Your responses:** You can't control someone else's actions, thoughts or feelings. But you can control how you react to what's happening, and look for ways to respond to hot button topics that won't escalate your anxiety or your anger.

- **Your investment:** In trying to control everything, you lose your ability to control anything! Instead, try to reduce your investment in the drama. Spend less time thinking about it, talking about it and engaging in it.

- **Your role in the conflict:** Step outside of your thoughts and feelings and consider how your actions and reactions look to others. Consider the impact of your actions, and honestly identify your role in the conflict. When you have your answer, see what you're willing to change.

Visit dummies.com for free access to great *For Dummies* content online.

Chapter 1

Conflict Resolution at Work

*Y*ou may love your family and friends but, truth be told, you spend much of your time with the people at work. Not getting along with co-workers or having members of your team at odds with one another can be stressful and distracting. In addition, problems in the workplace rarely stay at work; they can permeate every aspect of your life. So you need to take the time to understand what's behind a conflict, get beyond the surface issues and work to help find satisfying resolutions for everyone involved.

Settling differences effectively requires you to step back and look at the broader picture, be mindful of another person's point of view, and take into account peripheral factors that may be creating or provoking problems, like group dynamics or workplace norms.

In this chapter, I give you an overview of conflict resolution so you can successfully mediate problems in your workplace, whether those problems are between two individuals or within a larger group. I also tell you about additional conflict resolution resources you may have at your disposal.

Considering Common Contributors to Conflict

For the most part, workplace difficulties fall into common categories, such as

- ✔ Communication (and miscommunication)
- ✔ Employee attitudes
- ✔ Honesty
- ✔ Insubordination
- ✔ Treatment of others
- ✔ Work habits

Effectively addressing conflict takes into account the obvious surface issue, the emotional climate surrounding the topic, and your knowledge of the viewpoints of the people involved in the dispute. In this section, I provide insight into how differing perspectives can cause employees to feel like ships passing in the night. I also discuss emotions, touch on the importance of communication in your organisation, and look at group dynamics, including your role in the group.

Acknowledging differing perspectives

You and each of the employees on your team have a lens through which you see the world and one another. Everything you see, hear and say goes through your filter on the way in *and* on the way out. These filters determine how you present and receive information.

Your individual kaleidoscope is shaped by things like your personal history, education, values, culture and the roles you play in your life, both at work and at home. Everything you consider important works together to create your worldview. The same is true for your co-workers.

Values in this context are things like safety, respect, autonomy and recognition.

Being familiar with your employees' and colleagues' values helps you resolve conflicts. For example, say that two employees are having an argument over where to stack some binders.

If you can appreciate that one employee sees respect as paramount in his environment, and that his workspace is being encroached by his colleague with a lackadaisical attitude toward boundaries, you have a better chance of helping the two resolve the issue. Rather than swooping in to tell the pair that the binders they're arguing about should go on a shelf, you can facilitate a conversation about the real issue — respect. After you address the issue of respect, where the binders should go will be relatively easy to decide.

In Chapter 2, I go into more detail about filters, values and the emotions individuals bring to conflict.

Recognising emotions in others

Most organisations embrace positive emotions. Where managers often falter is in failing to recognise that every emotion — from upbeat to angry — is a clue to discovering people's personal values. Positive emotions are a sign that values are being met, while negative ones suggest that some work still needs to be done!

It's obvious that a situation has turned emotional when tears flow or an employee ratchets up the volume when he speaks, to the point that the entire office slips into an uncomfortable silence. What's a little more difficult is knowing what to do with such passionate responses. Emotional reactions are often seen as negative behaviour in just about any workplace, but if you spend some time investigating and interpreting them, you can get a leg up on how to resolve the trouble. Check out Chapter 2 for a complete discussion of emotions at work.

Handling communication mishaps

Communication makes the world go round, and the same is true for you and your employees. Word choice, tone of voice and body language all contribute to whether or not you understand each other.

Using vague or confusing language causes communication misfires. Phrases such as 'when you get a chance', 'several', or 'sometimes' don't accurately state what you really mean. Similarly, words like 'always' and 'never' can get you in trouble. Choosing your words wisely, and in a way that invites dialogue, makes for a less stressful work environment and models good communication. See Chapter 2 for more tips on communicating effectively.

Deciphering group dynamics

Two employees can completely understand each other and work like a well-oiled machine. Then a third co-worker joins the team, and now you have group dynamics in play. Wow, that changes everything! A team that's cohesive and meeting its goals can be exhilarating from management's perspective. But if cliques form and co-workers start looking for allies to enlist in power plays behind closed doors, communication breaks down.

Teams have a propensity to label members — the caretaker, the go-to guy, the historian and so on. Employees start to make assumptions based on the labelled roles, such as assuming that the go-to guy will happily accept any assignment you give him. Conjecture based on limited or selective information causes miscommunication, misunderstandings and, ultimately, conflict.

To address what happens when members of a group are undergoing difficulties, investigate how and when the problem started and determine if the problem stems from just a few staff members or if the impact is so great that you need to tackle the problem with the entire team. And flip to Chapter 3 for more information on the way group dynamics can contribute to conflict.

Assessing your own role

Something you're either doing or *not* doing may be causing friction on your team, and you may not even know what it is. Most people in conflict tend to spend more time thinking about what the other person is doing than looking at their own behaviour and attitudes toward the difficulty.

Chapter 4 outlines some of the common missteps that colleagues, and especially managers, make in their attempts to handle problems at work. I discuss ways you may be unwittingly pitting team members against each other, address the dreaded micromanaging accusation, and explain how underrepresenting your team to the higher-ups may unite them in a way that puts you at the centre of a storm.

Mediating like a Pro

When I meet with clients in conflict, I prefer to use a tried-and-true mediation process that looks at both the surface issues and the underlying causes for the difficulty. In this section, I show you why mediation is your best bet for a long-term solution and improved working relationship.

Following eight steps to a resolution

Using a solid process to mediate a meeting between co-workers in conflict gives you a foundation on which to manage and monitor the difficulty. Follow these steps from a professional mediation process:

1. **Do preliminary planning and setup:** Carefully investigate who's involved and what you believe the issues are, and invite the parties to discuss the matter with you. Provide a private, comfortable and confidential environment for the meeting.

2. **Greet and discuss the process:** Explain your role as a neutral facilitator and go over the ground rules, including your expectation for open minds and common courtesy.

3. **Share perspectives:** Give each person an opportunity to share her point of view and discuss the impact the conflict has had on her. Reflect, reframe and neutralise emotional content while honouring the spirit of what she's sharing.

4. **Build an agenda:** Allow both parties to create a list of topics (not solutions) they want to discuss. The list acts as a road map that keeps the discussion on track.

5. **Negotiate in good faith:** As co-workers discuss initial ideas for solutions, set the tone by listening to any and all ideas. Brainstorm and play out how suggestions might work and whether they satisfy what's most important to the employees.

6. **Hold private meetings as necessary:** Confidentially explore what's keeping each from moving forward, and discuss what each is willing to do (or ask for) in the spirit of progress and real resolution.

7. **Craft agreements:** Bring employees back together and let them share, if they so choose, any discoveries they made during the private meeting sessions. Begin to narrow down solutions and come to an agreement (with details!) on who will do what and when.

8. **Monitor follow-through:** Keep track of progress, address hiccups and refine as appropriate.

Facilitating a conversation between two people

Before you begin the mediation process, you need to consider the following:

- ✔ **A suitable meeting space:** You want the employees to feel comfortable enough in the meeting location to open up about the real issues. Meet in a place that has lots of privacy and is seen as neutral territory.

- ✔ **Confidentiality:** You need to build trust for a mediation conversation (see Chapter 6 for details on setting up a meeting), so agreeing to keep the conversation between the colleagues is a must, whether you act as mediator or bring in an outside expert.

- ✔ **Time and interruptions:** You probably want to set aside up to four hours to work through the issues, and you want to clear your schedule of other responsibilities so that the meeting isn't interrupted.

When you make the decision to mediate a conversation between feuding parties, a few things change for you. It's imperative that you walk a fine line between manager or colleague and mediator. As a manager, you have the power to make decisions; as a mediator, you have the power to put the onus on the employees and act as a neutral third party.

Practising the arts of reflecting and reframing an employee's point of view may be an initial challenge for you, but it's worth it in the end. Chapter 7 walks you through these steps and helps you keep your footing along the path of conflict resolution.

Negotiating a resolution to conflict starts with getting all the relevant information about the past on the table and ends with a clear definition of what the future could be. Get there by listening for what's really important to the parties involved and then asking directed, open-ended questions. In Chapter 8, I provide questions and cover the process of moving people through the negotiation stage of a mediated conversation.

The best solutions satisfy all parties involved and, perhaps more important, are lasting. Chapter 9 helps you work with your employees to develop good solutions and agreements.

Managing conflict with a team

If the conflict making its way through your organisation seems to affect each and every employee, suggesting, planning for and/or facilitating a team meeting may be the answer.

The more upfront preparation you do, the better your odds are for a fruitful outcome, so set yourself up for success by following a few simple tips:

- ✔ Decide whether you're neutral enough to facilitate the conversation. If not, look to a professional mediator or conflict resolution specialist to help.

- ✔ Consider broad details like your goals and how you'll develop milestones that quantify progress.

- ✔ Plan for smaller details, like exactly how you'll organise small group work and handle hecklers.

In Chapter 10, I discuss how to resolve conflict when larger groups are involved.

Following up and monitoring the situation takes some attention on your part. Look for signs of decreased tension and increases in work quality and quantity so that you can get out of the referee role and back into the position of managing the business you were hired to direct.

Tapping into Conflict Resolution Expertise

You don't have to go it alone when addressing conflict. And you don't need to jump in and attack the situation without first looking at the tools available to you. Create a customised approach by looking at what's already in place and then how to augment that with a little help from your friends.

The human resources (HR) department is an obvious place to start when you begin your search for advice and insight about a conflict. These personnel professionals can help you investigate an employee's work history and interpret company policy or employment law. They often lend a hand with customised trainings and can identify employee assistance programs such as counselling and addiction specialists.

They can also point you to other entities that may be able to help, including

- **Internal mediators and counsellors:** Common in large organisations and government agencies, internal mediators (also known as *shared neutrals* or *internal commissioners*) are individuals selected from different departments with various levels of authority. They're trained in mediation and are brought together to purposely create a diverse group perspective. Counsellors are usually employees in a company who provide a safe place to talk, vent and explore ideas.

- **Conflict resolution specialists and statutory authorities:** External conflict resolution specialists may be required if you can't resolve the conflict internally. Statutory bodies such as the Fair Work Commission or Employment Relations Authority provide opportunities for mediation for individuals who believe workplace rights and entitlements under applicable laws have been breached.

- **Unions:** If your company has a relationship with a union, you can always tap into its strength and problem-solving expertise.

Flip to Chapter 11 for more about internal resources you may be able to utilise in a conflict.

Chapter 2

Understanding What People Bring to Conflict

*E*ach person in your workplace is a complex system of past experiences, beliefs, values, opinions and emotions. Each has different ways of communicating, processing the things around him or her, and handling conflict.

This chapter helps you gain a better insight into the people on your team — why they see things the way they do, why they react to different people in different ways, and how their emotions can complicate the whole situation. You can start to understand how your colleagues' personal beliefs and attributes contribute to the team dynamic and sometimes contribute to conflict (which is normal, natural and inevitable, by the way) so that you can build better working relationships and a more productive working environment. You'll see the broader foundation of conflict and be more prepared to proactively reduce and perhaps prevent it.

Rediscovering Communication

Good communication is the hallmark of a productive working relationship. Easier said than done, right? Even when you believe you're being crystal clear, it's possible that the other person doesn't understand what you're really trying to say.

This happens for a variety of reasons, including differences in goals, misunderstandings with language, ambiguous body language and misinterpretations of tone of voice.

Changing the goal of communication

In conflict, goals for communication often turn destructive. If someone in your group enters into a conversation for the sole purpose of proving that she's right, making the other person feel bad or establishing that the other person is an incompetent fool, the conflict is likely to get worse.

Reaching agreement is commonly thought of as the goal of communication, but this misconception is often one of the most unnecessary causes of conflicts. Instead, focus on creating understanding — and understanding doesn't mean agreeing. It isn't necessary for the two people in conflict to see eye to eye and walk away holding hands, but it's helpful if they can talk to each other respectfully, feel heard by each other, and gain a greater understanding of the situation and the other person.

The old cliché 'agree to disagree' may be coming to mind. In a way, this saying is both accurate and inaccurate. The two people in the conflict may end their discussion on this note, and that's fine as long as they both put forth a 100-per-cent effort to listen and understand each other. Unfortunately, most people use this saying as a quick way to end a conversation. They're tired of trying to talk with the other person so they agree to disagree as a polite way of brushing off the other person. That's not what striving for understanding is about.

Ultimately, if two people have a real and productive conversation where they both listen and feel heard, they'll probably find more in common with each other and find more points to agree on. Changing the goal of communication is a new way to think about it and, even if you're not directly involved in the conflict, if you shift your thinking, you'll have a head start on working with employees to solve their issues.

Choosing words carefully: The importance of language

One of the most common contributors to miscommunication is language. The words you use can lead to misinterpretations and negative reactions, either because you choose words that don't accurately express what you're trying to say or you use words that the listener finds inappropriate or insulting. In some cases, the miscommunication is simply a matter of *semantics* (the meaning and interpretation of words).

Making sure you're on the same page

Words are slippery things, and the same word can have different meanings for different people. The best ways to avoid misunderstandings are to be specific and to get creative. Take more time in a conversation, choose your words carefully and ask clarifying questions. If you suspect semantics are getting in the way, take a moment to define the word in question. State what that word means to you, and ask the other person what it means to her. This clarification could shed light on the disagreement.

When starting a conversation, try to avoid misunderstandings by giving thought to what information you're trying to relay or gather, and then formulate a statement or question that meets that goal. For example, asking a colleague to respect you isn't as clear as asking her to respect you by not playing practical jokes on you. Telling your boss that you want time off isn't as clear as requesting leave for the week of 1 January.

You can also get creative and find other ways to get your message across. If words are keeping people from a shared understanding, try a different method of communication. Visual aids like photos, maps, charts and diagrams can be tremendously helpful. In some situations you may find that a demonstration or tutorial clarifies a point.

Being precise

Using words or phrases that are vague or too open to interpretation can cause problems. If you're using one of the following words or phrases, consider whether you can be more precise:

- Sometimes
- In a timely manner
- As needed
- To my satisfaction
- A few
- Several

> ✓ Often
>
> ✓ Frequently
>
> ✓ When you get a chance

Be proactive and use specifics whenever possible. If you have an expectation that the sales receipts need to be turned in 'at the end of the day', say that what you really mean is 'by 5.30 pm each and every day'. Being specific avoids confusion and uncertainty.

Avoiding inflammatory language

Using the wrong language can make a good situation bad or a bad situation worse. By choosing inflammatory words to get a message across, you can easily sound insulting, insensitive, hurtful or just plain mean. Some inflammatory words, such as name-calling, are very obvious. Calling someone stupid, lazy or incompetent can get you in trouble, not only with your team or manager but also with the human resources department!

Beyond the obvious, some words are just easier for a listener to hear. For example, if an employee or colleague approaches you and says, 'I hate my job', you'll probably have a negative reaction. If the same employee instead says, 'I'm dissatisfied with my job', your reaction would be quite different. Some words have a negative impact, and the trick to getting a more positive reaction from listeners is to find more neutral words that they won't find offensive. I provide hints on neutralising language in Chapter 7.

Body language: Others' and your own

Another important element in an individual's communication arsenal is body language. Body language goes beyond obvious gestures (like showing someone your appreciation when he cuts you off in traffic!) and encompasses everything people do physically while they're in a conversation.

Body language that's open and encouraging includes

> ✓ Facing the person who's speaking
>
> ✓ Making good eye contact
>
> ✓ Nodding occasionally
>
> ✓ Having arms in an open position rather than crossed in front of the chest

Body language can also be closed and discourage communication. The following will shut down the conversation and probably earn you a reputation for being rude:

- ✔ Not looking at the person speaking

- ✔ Rolling your eyes

- ✔ Having an expressionless face, frowning or squinting to indicate the speaker isn't making any sense

- ✔ Staring off into space

- ✔ Turning your back to the speaker

Pay attention to your group and make note of body language during tense or heated conversations. Do the same when things are going well and note the difference.

Be aware of the nonverbal cues you're giving off in the workplace, and be aware of the nonverbal cues you're getting from everyone else. Clenched fists, tightness in the shoulders and increased breathing can all indicate stress, whereas a relaxed posture, leaning back in the chair and a smile can mean happiness and contentment. What do these gestures say about the work environment, your team and yourself? When you know what to look for, you can tell a lot about someone's day before she even says a word.

Use body language as a clue to discern what may be going on, but don't use it exclusively. If a co-worker walks into the office one day, doesn't say hello and immediately sits down at her desk, maybe she's mad at you — or maybe she has a very busy day ahead and wants to stay focused. Making some assumptions about body language is fine, but check out those assumptions before acting or reacting badly. For more information on assumptions, see Chapter 3.

Discerning tone of voice

A largely under-recognised yet critical part of verbal communication is tone of voice. *How* something is said — either the tone used or the inflection given — can completely change the meaning of the words. Without knowing whether the speaker's intent is to be funny, sarcastic, serious or sincere, a person may respond inappropriately. This often happens to people who communicate predominantly in writing. The written word leaves tone of voice open to interpretation, and you don't want to learn that lesson the hard way.

Depending on the kinds of interactions you have with employees, you may or may not be familiar with their style of communication. If you have a new team member, it may take some time before everyone can accurately identify when that person is being serious and when she's being sarcastic. Some guesswork comes into play, but the important thing is to be aware of the role tone of voice plays in communication and, ultimately, in conflict. Tone may be the whole reason for a dispute.

Knowing some of the finer points of communication helps you consider conflict causes that go beyond the obvious reasons. Rather than letting the interpretation fester, address tone early on by asking a few questions to bring awareness to the speaker. For example, if I'm talking with someone who has an edge to her voice, I may ask if she's having a bad day or if she's upset with me. Sometimes the answer is 'yes' (to one of my questions) and sometimes the speaker is simply unaware that she's coming across that way. This is a two-way street, so feel free to ask if the way you're speaking is getting in the way of the listener understanding your point.

Figuring Out Why People Think the Way They Do

People are unique in the ways they receive and process information, and you could spend many years trying to analyse your team. But to makes things a bit simpler, for now consider this section's practical overview of what makes individuals tick.

Values: Understanding what's important to people

Everyone has a set of core *values* — things that are fundamentally important to them. These values, which are sometimes called *interests*, are the underlying beliefs and principles that individuals carry around with them every single day, and they differ from person to person.

Being aware of the fact that values are common motivators for people gives you greater insight into why certain conflicts happen. Identifying the values in a conflict helps you find resolution to the conflict. When the conversation changes from individual positions to what's most important to everyone, you and your team can expand your options to include solutions that work for everyone.

People don't have just one core value; they have a whole set of values with varying degrees of importance. These values affect how they act, react, and interact with their environments. Values can include accountability, control, family, honesty and security. Understanding other people's values can help you make the connection between a surface issue and a deeper motivation.

In my experience, some values are common, and then a handful of values are almost always at the heart of a workplace conflict. Take a closer look at these and see if you can identify any of them within your team:

- **Acceptance:** People who value acceptance want to be part of the team. They want to feel like an equal, be in on information as soon as it's out there, and generally feel a sense of belonging.

- **Accomplishment:** People who value accomplishment love it when the job is done and there's a finished product. Taking something from nothing, working it all the way through, and not giving up are important to them.

- **Autonomy:** Those who look for autonomy place a high value on being accountable to self over others. They like to work at their own pace, free from oversight and the influence of supervisors. They may enjoy working as part of a team but prefer to be fully responsible and accountable, demonstrating that they can be trusted to get the job done.

- **Competence:** Those who value competence may place a strong emphasis on knowledge, skills and training. These folks like to do the job right the first time and look for others to do the same. They want to believe that management has matched the right person to the job at hand. They may be quick to complain if they feel someone is falling short on their responsibilities, but that's because at their core they care about the quality of the work.

- **Control:** These folks have a need to know all the details, and it's important to them to orchestrate every aspect of larger projects. Managing or working with them, you may appreciate that they're able to see the big picture, but you may notice that they risk getting bogged down in the details.

- ✔ **Cooperation:** 'We're all responsible for the work that gets done around here', says the person who values cooperation. These people look toward the sharing of information, tasks and details to further the ends of the organisation they work for. They believe that people are better and more successful working together than individually. Go team!

- ✔ **Recognition:** Those who value recognition may place a high value on giving and receiving credit for a job well done. They thrive on compliments, and they may have awards and certificates plastered on their walls. A pat on the back goes a long way with these team members. For them knowing they did a good job is not always enough; they want something to validate the results and will work hard to get it.

- ✔ **Respect:** Respect is one of the most common values and yet one of the most elusive to explain. Respect in the workplace can be acknowledging someone's expertise, validating a person's contribution to the group, or simply not stealing someone's lunch out of the refrigerator. On a basic level, those who value respect treat others in a way that doesn't diminish their self-worth.

These values and others show up at work every day. How someone reacts to a situation can give you a clue about her values. For example, if an employee becomes upset when a customer is rude to her, that employee probably values respect or common courtesy. If your boss gives you a raise because you always get your work done by the deadlines, your boss may value responsibility. If you feel frustrated and angry because a colleague lied to you, you may value honesty.

Values are unique to the individual, so don't assume you've automatically identified the right value for a co-worker, or that you can label someone with just one value. If three staff members get upset because their meeting started 15 minutes late, that doesn't mean they all value the same thing. One may be upset because starting a meeting late is disrespectful of his time or because he values order. Another may be upset because family is the most important thing to her and she's missing time she could be spending with her family. And the third person may want everyone to show up for the meeting on time because that's how adults show they're responsible and accountable. All may additionally value honesty, which they feel has been violated, because previous agreements stressed that meetings should start on time.

When you're dealing with a conflict at work, a person's values show up in two ways:

- ✔ A particular issue becomes a problem for an individual based on her values.

- ✔ The people involved in the problem take certain positions because of their values.

Filters: Sifting through information

Each person has her own filters or lens through which she sees the world. Everything she sees, hears and says has to go through not only her own filter but through the filters of everyone she interacts with. These filters can colour, distort or amplify the information in both positive and negative ways.

Filters are a manifestation of self-identity, which is how people see themselves in the world. It's your belief of who you are as a person and the characteristics you place on yourself, whether you identify as being smart, funny, conservative, law-abiding, forgetful or loving. Contributors to self-identity include personal history, culture, values, roles (within families and with friends, for example) and education.

All these things create self-identity and, collectively, they help answer the question of why people say and do the things they say and do. (Because people are individuals, that's why.) In the workplace, you have a collection of people with different histories, values, cultures and roles working together. Differences in opinions, work approaches, communication styles and expectations are inevitable. Strive to understand everyone's diversity, and use it to create a strong, effective and respectful work environment. Differences are the one thing everyone has in common!

History: Operating from the past

People use past experiences to predict the future. If Joe the delivery guy is always 30 minutes late, you're going to assume the next time you place an order that he'll be 30 minutes late. If he's been late the last seven times, why would you think he'd be on time now?

This phenomenon for using the past to indicate the future is both useful and limiting. You can draw from your experiences and knowledge to be productive. For example, a receptionist usually knows when staff members are in their offices and can refer calls and clients appropriately, or a supervisor may know that the majority of her team prefers to take a vacation day on the Friday before a three-day weekend and plans accordingly.

Viewing the future as a continuation of the past can be dangerous in some cases because doing so doesn't allow for change. Perhaps you hear comments from colleagues such as, 'Susan never gets her reports in on time', or, 'Steve always comes in late'. When you hear these comments, don't accept them as the unwavering truth for future behaviour. If these behaviours are undesirable and you want them to stop, consider what it will take to change the situation and make the future look different from the past. This may mean having individual conversations with employees, or bringing two or more employees together for a discussion. Chapter 5 gives you additional tools to assess the situation.

People have very different past experiences. What you know to be true because of a previous experience may not be true for someone else. Just because you've had a bad interaction with a co-worker doesn't mean that everyone else in the office has.

When differences of opinion escalate to major conflict, co-workers may lose faith in one another and form patterns of negative associations. These feelings can be compounded by unsuccessful attempts to correct the behaviour. Hopelessness sets in, trust is lost and individuals become unhappy, disillusioned and dissatisfied. If you're part of or you've inherited (or created) a team like this, all is not lost. The good news is that you can change it! State that current behaviour or patterns of behaviour are opportunities to change. Be clear with directives, investigate barriers to change, and address issues early as ways to demonstrate your belief that what has happened in the past doesn't have to be the recipe for the future.

Considering the Importance of Emotions

Many people believe that work is work and that emotions have no place in a professional setting. You hear people refer to emotions as a sign of weakness, and employees who can bottle up their emotional reactions and behave like robots on the job are often praised. So if that's the goal, try a mental experiment. Strip all emotion out of your workplace. No anger, fear, frustration or jealousy — this sounds great, right? Of course, you also have to take away pride in a job well done, enthusiasm for the mission, inspiration to provide a better service and satisfaction in an accomplishment. The workplace void of emotion is a collection of automatons going to work every day out of need or habit; such an atmosphere lacks joy, admiration, curiosity or wonder. That sounds rather depressing and boring. Oh sorry — those are emotions, too.

Get past the notion of never needing or wanting emotions in the workplace. Focus on how to productively and professionally contribute to and influence the emotional climate in the workplace, which allows you to get the best out of yourself and those in your team. To discover how to do that, read on.

Listening to what emotions tell you

In the workplace, you'll see strong emotions around values like security, survival and anything that impacts people's ability to maintain their basic needs. You'll also see strong reactions around issues of professionalism, accomplishment or reputation from individuals whose sense of self is closely tied to their occupation. Keep in mind that what's happening *at* work may not stem *from* work. An employee may be feeling that core values in her personal life are at risk, which in turn can trigger negative emotions on the job.

Anger is a more complex emotion than most people realise. Anger has a natural tendency to mask or overshadow other emotions a person may be feeling. For example, a co-worker may be angry about a joke that made her look bad. If you dig deeper, her core emotion is embarrassment, and the anger is the outward expression of it. This is true for a lot of emotions, including fear, worry, disappointment and confusion. Peel back the layers of the conflict and the emotions to get at what's really happening for that person. Ask open-ended questions like those in Chapter 8 to identify what's important so you can find a more accurate solution.

Dealing with emotional intensity and impact

Not all emotions are equal in intensity. Some are mild and unassuming, while others are strong and imposing. The intensity of an emotion may be a clear indication of how important that topic or subject is to someone.

The intensity of emotions can play a large role in the escalation of conflict. Visualise a conflict escalator — the higher you go on the escalator, the more intense and serious the conflict and emotions are. Also realise that the higher up on the escalator you go, the harder it is to come down.

Anger is a natural response to many negative conflicts; it prepares the mind and body to protect and defend itself. Therefore, anger is sometimes necessary for survival. However, far too often in conflict situations, anger takes a person up the conflict escalator and ends up making the situation worse instead of better.

 Be aware of the emotional climate in your workplace, and address medium-intensity emotions and conflicts early on. Addressing a situation when someone is agitated is easier than when she's irate. Low-intensity emotions or conflicts probably don't need your intervention. Let people have a bad day or be frustrated with a client's demands without investigating further. Keep an eye on things, and if you see a situation turn a corner or become worse, you always have the option to act.

Finally, be aware of the cycle of strong emotion. When people reach the very top of the conflict escalator, they're in crisis mode, and their emotions make it nearly impossible for them to think clearly. Reasoning and logic are easier for someone to access either before she gets to the point of crisis or after the crisis is over and she's had an opportunity to relax. After a blow-up at work, don't try to reason and negotiate with the person right then and there. Be aware of the cycle and give the individual some time to cool down.

Acknowledging and processing difficult emotions in your team

Positive emotions are accepted and encouraged in the workplace, but negative emotions cause dread, discomfort or panic in everyone around them.

Simply wanting these emotions to go away won't bring peace and happiness into your workplace. On the contrary, the emotions will continue to cause you and your organisation conflict until you help deal with them.

But most people — managers and co-workers alike — are unequipped to handle emotions. They can tell when someone is getting emotional, but the ability to accurately identify or handle the emotion is another story. No matter how long you've been employed, you've probably experienced the disruptive impact of negative emotions in the workplace, so focusing now on how to handle situations when they arise will give you a leg up on creating and contributing to a more productive team.

First, be a good listener. Hear what the person has to say, and don't be compelled to fix the problem or offer solutions. Often, if a person can simply talk about what she's feeling, she can identify the emotion and gain the ability to move forward all on her own. Sometimes just allowing someone to get her concerns off her chest can resolve the conflict. Who hasn't benefited from a good talk, laugh or cry about a situation? Getting it out means she can sift through all the emotions and you can help her discover what's really bothering her so she can create a fix that matches the problem. For tips on how to demonstrate that you're listening, see Chapter 7.

While you're showing that you're listening, help your employee or colleague identify the source of her emotion by asking open-ended questions like those found in Chapter 8. Helping someone understand why she's feeling frustrated or upset can bring her some relief. In particular, if you sense a strong degree of fear, uncertainty or anxiety, you may want to look for something that has threatened her sense of security or caused a significant sense of loss. Things like budget cuts, downsizing or fear of losing an important business account often cause these emotions.

Responding to Conflict

People react to and manage conflict very differently. Three people in the same situation may have three distinctly different reactions. And to make matters more complex, not only do people act differently in conflict, but the same person may respond one way in one situation and react another way in a different situation.

Methods for managing conflict vary from person to person and situation to situation. Each method has its own distinct benefits when used in the right situations. Following are some common conflict management styles that people in your team may use and hints on how you can address them.

Giving in

This technique simply lets people have what they want. When someone who tends to give in finds herself in conflict, she's prone to sacrifice her own opinions or requests just to keep the peace.

You may work with someone who's considered the ultimate team player. Everyone knows if they need help with something, they can go to this person because she never says no. Even when she has work up to her ears, she finds a way to accommodate requests. Above all, this person wants peace in the office. She doesn't want to hurt anyone's feelings and she'll do anything to preserve working relationships, even at the expense of her health, happiness or sanity!

The person who gives in rarely makes waves at work and is often considered by higher-ups (sometimes incorrectly) to be the easiest employee to manage. But managing an employee who doesn't put up a fight is more complicated than it sounds. Be extra sensitive to whether this employee is being overworked or taken advantage of. She may not verbalise her dissatisfaction with how she's being treated, and she may repress her emotions to the point of explosion. She's the type of employee who will up and quit one day, and you'll have no idea why. Check in frequently and let her know that it's okay to say no when she's overwhelmed. You may also need to help her set new boundaries and create more balanced relationships with her co-workers.

Avoiding the fight

This is the 'flight' portion of the old adage 'fight or flight'. Rather than deal with the conflict, this person would rather avoid it altogether. She has a fairly low tolerance for conflict and places a high importance on safety and comfort.

You may have someone on your team who calls in sick frequently, prefers to work alone or at home, or would rather pass off problems or difficult conversations onto you or her boss. Her sensitivity to conflict is high, and she may have trouble working with more aggressive or demanding individuals. It's not uncommon for these employees to be passive aggressive at times, asserting their power in ways that don't involve face-to-face confrontation, like communicating disagreements by email, not passing along information to make co-workers look bad or just not showing up to an important meeting.

An employee who avoids conflict needs encouragement to engage in difficult conversations, whether with you or with a co-worker. If you want her to open up to you, make sure she knows that you're receptive and ready to listen. If she has concerns, such as confidentiality, find ways to reassure her that it's safe to talk with you.

You may also want to increase her exposure to productive conflict. Holding staff meetings that allow for a free flow of ideas, some of which may be contradictory, is a way to place her in the middle of conflict without experiencing the force of it directly. Make sure the conversation is open and respectful; it helps if team members trust one another well enough to be honest without taking any disagreements personally.

Fighting it out

These employees have no problem standing up for themselves. They're aggressive when confronted with conflict, and they may be the ones who start it in the first place. They may even view conflict as a game, and they enjoy competition because it's an opportunity to win. They're comfortable arguing and are persistent in fighting for what they think is right.

Often viewed as go-getters, these employees are focused and driven. It's not uncommon for them to be the most productive members on the team. When they find themselves disagreeing with someone, they can be insulting or dismissive without even meaning to be. If their aggression remains unchecked, they can become the bullies in the office.

You may have to expand a fighter's focus to include the people around her. Help her concentrate on solutions that meet everyone's needs, not just her own. Let her know that working together allows her to reach her professional goals faster than her working alone. Do this in a private conversation in which you set an expectation for her new way of thinking. It's my experience that trying to swim upstream all the time only results in water up your nose, so point out that working against someone takes up valuable energy that could be used for everyone's benefit — especially hers!

Compromising

If you have a compromiser working with you, you'll notice that she isn't afraid of conflict but that she doesn't like to spend a lot of time on it, either. Conflict is a bother to her, a distraction from the real work that needs to get done. She tends to look for a quick and fair resolution. She's the first to suggest splitting a disputed dollar amount right down the middle, or she may support a proposal that gives everyone a little of what they want.

You should encourage an employee who jumps to a compromise quickly to look at the larger picture. Splitting something down the middle is fine in some situations, but sometimes that's not possible or advantageous. Help people with this style expand their thinking to include what it is that each person really wants. (Read the earlier section 'Values: Understanding what's important to people' for ideas to get past the surface issues.)

Working together

Some people really enjoy working with others. In all aspects of their lives, they'd rather work or interact with people than be alone. As employees, they're very social and enjoy a good, thorough conversation. You may notice that they seek out the opinions of others when making decisions and often get into long discussions with colleagues because they enjoy collaborating and sharing ideas. They approach conflict in a similar way — they want to work through the conflict by discussing all the possible solutions, looking for the perfect answer.

Working together, although great at creating and supporting relationships among employees, doesn't work well when quick decisions need to be made. It's often difficult for people with this style to know when the discussion is over and when it's time to make a decision. When working in groups, these employees may alienate or exhaust peers who prefer action over words.

One way to help is to provide focus. Given the information they have available to them, what decisions can they make now? It can also be useful to provide boundaries and deadlines well in advance. Give them structure with clear expectations and a little additional time so they can gather information, but let them know the point when the talking needs to stop and they must make a decision.

Chapter 3

Determining How Groups Contribute to Conflict

. . . .

In This Chapter

▶ Identifying how your employees fit within your organisation

▶ Highlighting common areas of conflict within teams

▶ Avoiding negative group behaviours

. . . .

*P*ut two or more people in a work setting and you're bound to have conflict. And, whether you wear a white tie, a blue shirt or a uniform, your workplace has naturally and artificially formed groups that add characteristics to the work environment and, ultimately, to conflict. But, when working as part of a team, you know that groups are essential!

Created based on similar job assignments (like the accounting department) or pulled together based on skill sets (like a selected task force), groups are required to get the work done. Teams can work like well-oiled machines that win awards, exceed sales projections, solve what seem like insurmountable problems and build elaborate buildings in record time. So if groups have the capacity to do such great things, what is it about them that causes conflict?

In this chapter, I share how the company, its culture and the phenomenon of group dynamics all have the potential to turn an otherwise functioning group into a fragmented team of distracted individuals.

Observing Your Organisation's Culture

Conflict between two employees is one thing, but when conflict is between employees and the organisation it's a whole other issue. When employees are up in arms, consider how the organisation itself may be contributing to conflict. Start by looking at your enterprise and consider its culture.

Some examples of different kinds of workplace cultures include:

- ✔ **Top-down, military-style organisations.** These often have a very clear hierarchy, and stress the importance of structure and protocol. Decisions are made by those with power and rank. A structured company is a difficult work environment for people who prefer a more relaxed and flexible workplace or find value in the discussions that take place before decisions are made.

- ✔ **Production or assembly-line companies.** These focus on the individual and her role in the company. Like cogs in a wheel, employees are responsible for completing their part of a task so that everything continues to function properly. Employees who value creativity and like to do new and different things every day often don't appreciate this way of doing business and may feel stifled and unappreciated.

- ✔ **Organisations with a looser configuration of employees.** These put less emphasis on teamwork and more on individual achievement. Companies that have independent salespeople, for example, provide a lot of autonomy to their employees and focus more on the end goal than how the goal is achieved. This kind of environment doesn't work well for people who are motivated by collaboration and structure.

- ✔ **Establishments that prioritise people and ideas over products.** In these companies, titles and rank aren't important, and everyone has a vote in what happens. These environments don't work well for people who want to work independently or who don't appreciate a 20-minute discussion every time a decision needs to be made.

In addition to your company's culture, it has a distinct personality that's a combination of the culture and the unique personalities of its employees at any given time. Conflict comes into play when the culture and organisational personality don't fit with the values or needs of one or more staff members.

Some employees expend a lot of energy trying to either fit into a workplace or make the workplace fit them. When neither possibility works, they have two options: Create a change to meet their needs or live within the structure that exists. If the conflict over culture is extreme and unworkable, the company may not be the right one for that employee — and that's okay.

Identifying the organisational focus

Your organisation has a goal, which is also called its purpose or mission statement — essentially, its reason for existing. This focus could be related to the kind of work environment you're in — corporate, business, government, non-profit, public service and so on — or it could depend on the philosophies and strategies of the leadership within your company, the management team, the board of directors or the advisory council.

Each employee in your organisation also has goals or reasons for going to work every day. How the goal of the whole organisation fits with the goals of individual employees can explain why some employees stay with a company for 40 years and others hightail it out in the first week. The difference in focus can be one source of conflict between employees and the organisation.

The scope of your company can also cause conflict. If the focus is too broad, some employees may become confused and uncertain about what direction the company is going. A non-profit that wants to help everyone in the community with every need will end up with tired and overwhelmed employees. Equally, if the focus is too narrow, it can limit employee potential and miss out on ideas that contribute to its prosperity.

Considering hiring or promoting practices

If you're a manager, being absolutely certain you're hiring or promoting the right person is impossible; however, you need to consider a few intangible qualifications for a potential employee in order to keep possible conflicts at bay. Set aside the obvious criteria — like education, experience and general ability to do the job — and then take some time to focus on how a new hire can affect a group.

Any change in personnel has a direct impact on a team. In a small business with only a handful of employees, everyone will be affected by a change. In larger corporations, those who work most directly with the new employee are most affected. Whatever the situation, consider who's going to have the most contact or interaction with the new hire, and think about what traits in a potential employee are the most compatible with your current team.

Consider having your team's work styles assessed. You can easily find tools and assessments (online, in bookstores or by hiring a specialist) to determine the strengths of each of your team members — and the exercise doesn't have to feel like a dreaded trip to the dentist. Not only will the assessment help you consider the traits and personalities you need from a new team member, but it also benefits employees, who need to work together on future projects.

Promoting an employee can be a little trickier than hiring someone new. You still want to consider the individual personality of the employee you're considering promoting, but you also need to be aware of how others will feel about the co-worker being promoted. Anger, jealousy and disappointment are common reactions in employees who have *not* been chosen for promotions and, no matter how fair the decision may have been, those reactions may still be present no matter whom you choose to promote from within.

Be available to help others process the change. You can listen to those who are disappointed without necessarily having to do anything about it. You aren't required to justify your decision or act on their concern, but giving them a chance to say they disagree may help them put the issue behind them. (If you're not sure how to listen without acting, practise some of the tips I give you in Chapter 7.)

Considering how your company adapts to change

The important thing for any manager or colleague to remember is how dramatic *any* change can be for a workplace. Recognise the impact and address it quickly and effectively. Change can bring up fear, uncertainty and stress for employees who are concerned about how the decisions will directly affect them, and they're relying on the organisation to provide them with accurate and up-to-date information when it's available. Do just that.

When a substantial change in the workplace is going to occur, consider the following:

- ✔ Who will be affected by the change?
- ✔ Who needs to be involved in the decision-making?
- ✔ How will those who are most affected have a voice in the decisions?
- ✔ What can you do to minimise rumours and inaccurate information?
- ✔ How much of what you know can you share with your colleagues and team?
- ✔ What is the best method for sharing information?

After you determine what you can share and the best method for sharing, be consistent. You can create calm in the storm by keeping people informed on a regular basis. Even if nothing has changed since the last time you spoke with team members, you can keep them focused by letting them know that you'll tell them *what* you can, *when* you can, and that you're keeping them in mind during the transition.

From the opposite perspective, what happens when a group or team within an organisation is more open and excited about change than the organisation itself? Consider how an organisation's resistance to change affects its employees. As staff create new and innovative ideas within an old, conservative structure, clashes can occur, valuable employees may leave and others will be less willing to take on new projects or even give their best to existing assignments.

If you're faced with such a position in a management role, acknowledge that you're in the middle. Do what you can to work within the structure that exists, listen to your team's concerns and brainstorm with them to determine what you're willing to do on their behalf.

When you experience a conflict caused by change, prepare to do some damage control. Keep in mind that you're not 100 per cent responsible for your employees' happiness, and pleasing everyone may not be possible, but consider a few of these ideas to help ease the tension:

- ✔ **Assess the fallout.** Find out which employees have been negatively affected by the change and how they're taking it.

- ✔ **Give people a voice.** You can accomplish this in a variety of ways, including person-to-person meetings, anonymous surveys and suggestion boxes.

- ✔ **Address concerns whenever possible.** Listening to perspectives and acknowledging the reality of the situation is often enough to get people back on track.

- ✔ **Allow whatever control is possible.** If people are asking for small, manageable changes that can be implemented, consider doing so.

- ✔ **If necessary, bring in a professional.** If the change has caused more conflict than you or your organisation can handle on its own, consider bringing in help.

Recognising Team Dynamics

When the members of a group or team work closely together, certain dynamics start to surface. Those dynamics can be positive and productive (for example, when everyone is on the same page and they blow deadlines out of the water) or negative and counterproductive (when a team doesn't see eye to eye and the work stops). A number of factors can affect the energy of your team. In the following sections, I tell you about some common ones.

Dealing with mismatched expectations

Everyone in the workplace has expectations. Those expectations can be concrete, like not parking in the areas reserved for the retail customers, or less tangible, like receiving respect from your colleagues. Conflict in groups comes into play when all the team members think they have the same expectations, but they really don't.

You may expect that your colleagues and employees will arrive on time, take their breaks as scheduled and leave on time. If one of your employees doesn't have that same expectation and decides to work more flexible hours, the two of you have mismatched expectations and a potential problem.

As soon as you get an inkling that someone's expectations are different from yours or from other members of the team:

> ✔ Ask each person to state his expectation and to expand on how he came to that point of view.

> ✔ Be clear about your expectations and the impact of not meeting them.

Acknowledging assigned and assumed roles

Groups tend to create official and unofficial roles for members. Much like a family or a sports team, individual employees take on certain responsibilities based on the needs of both the group and the person. After a role has been established, the group then relies on that member to fill that role.

Some roles — like a formal job description or a role specifically related to an assigned task — are officially handed down from the company. Other roles are self-selected — for example, maybe you enjoy planning parties, and you've taken it upon yourself to arrange all the upcoming birthday celebrations for the office. Now you're 'the party planner'.

Some roles are unofficially assigned to an individual by the rest of the group. You may have a colleague who's a particularly empathetic and compassionate listener. Other employees with a problem go to him because they know that they can share their problems and he'll listen. He's now 'the counsellor'.

These roles, whether assigned or assumed, have an impact on both the individual and the group. When things are going well and everyone is happy with their roles, operations run smoothly. When employees become unhappy with their roles, you see conflict. Negative emotions — like resentment, irritation and anger — often build in the person who no longer wants a particular role, and his dissatisfaction becomes more noticeable.

Times of transition can cause conflict because of the uncertainty involved. When an employee leaves, all his existing roles need to be filled. This includes roles that aren't attached to his job description but still impact the group. Co-workers may automatically assume the new person can fill all roles because he's the replacement, but the new person may not be happy with this imposed assignment because he doesn't think it's his responsibility. If you can, consider adding assumed roles to the new hire's job description, or divvying up the responsibilities among your team as a way to ensure that all tasks and responsibilities are covered.

Redefining power

The most easily understood indication of power in the workplace is title or hierarchy. Roles such as the CEO, the owner, the HR director, the boss or the manager are common representations of the traditional view of power. Beyond title or position within the organisation, however, power comes from other sources:

- ✔ Physical attributes, such as gender, appearance and age

- ✔ Mental attributes, such as aptitudes, language and problem-solving

- ✔ Skills, such as industry-specific skills, verbal or written communication skills, and interpersonal skills

- ✔ Experience, such as knowledge of the field and years with the company

- ✔ Status, such as money, education, and social or professional networks

Don't kid yourself and think that power only rests at the top. In one way or another, every single person in your organisation has some power because power is crucial to accomplishing work.

Clout associated with job skills and performance has a significant impact on the quality and quantity of work that gets done. Sources of power that relate to job performance, like the ability to persuade or the ability to track complicated details, are critical. Employees who constructively use their power are invaluable members of teams.

Power becomes problematic, however, when it isn't balanced. When a person or group has too much or too little power, team dynamics suffer and conflict is likely to arise.

Too much power

Be aware when power starts to become destructive — especially if you have a power-seeking group. Unchecked power coupled with a complete disregard for others is never a good combination. (See the 'Groups Behaving Badly' section later in this chapter for examples of negative group dynamics.)

So before someone on your team successfully builds his army of doom, take a few minutes to consider these power-balancing techniques:

- ✔ **Be a good role model.** As a manager or colleague, you always have an opportunity to model positive behaviour. Treat everyone respectfully and equally. Listen to the ideas of others and let them know that their opinions matter. Never assume that someone on your team doesn't have a great solution to a problem that's outside of his area of expertise.

- ✔ **Be aware of emerging power imbalances in the office.** Address negative, counterproductive or manipulative behaviour early. A private conversation with the offending employee is always a good first step.

- ✔ **Help your employees and colleagues use their power for good, not evil.** Power derived from job skills and performance can be channelled to help everyone, not just an individual at the expense of others. Point out the personal benefit in achieving group accomplishments in addition to individual accomplishments.

- ✔ **If you can pinpoint a leader, focus your energy on getting him to work with you.** He already has influence over a group of employees who could be valuable contributors if only everyone would get on the same page. Address the issue upfront, listen to his perspective, and see if you can refocus his power instead of simply squashing him (as tempting as that may be). He could become an invaluable asset to you.

- ✔ **Encourage participation from everyone, and make sure those seeking power don't take over.** Create an equal playing field for all employees by bringing everyone together at the same time, not just the employees in the power-seeking group. This method allows you to give everyone a voice, not just the group. (For more tips on facilitating a meeting of this nature, see Chapter 10.)

Too little power

Just as excessive power can be problematic, so can a lack of power. Employees who feel as though they have no control over their situation can easily become disengaged and unhappy. A lack of power to change or affect a situation significantly diminishes motivation, causes poor job performance, increases sick leave and potentially increases employee turnover.

When employees lose power or control over a situation, try the following:

- ✓ **Give your employees a forum to vent their frustration.** A private meeting with you will help them voice concerns and dissatisfaction.

- ✓ **Help them find things they can control.** These things could include other aspects of their job or how they want to respond to the situation, in either actions or words.

- ✓ **Provide support and look for resources if needed.** Be there for your colleagues and employees, as a stable presence who knows and understands what they're going through. When necessary, help them through difficult times by finding resources like a conflict coach, counselling service or government agency.

Groups Behaving Badly

Groups that work well are an important component of the workplace. Often, nothing is more satisfying from a managerial perspective than the positive energy of a group accomplishing goals. On the other hand, groups that start behaving badly can become an absolute nightmare.

When employees join forces against each other, spread rumours, make false assumptions and gossip, these actions can deplete morale and breed conflict. The following sections detail how staff associations can cause problems.

Joining cliques

I'm no sociologist, but I know enough about the workplace to know that people are social creatures by nature, and that when they take on new jobs they seek out other people who will show them the ropes and help them assimilate.

Groups — or cliques — form at work for a number of reasons, including shared interests, similar personalities or proximity in working environments. Whatever the motivation employees have for attaching themselves to co-workers, the attachment has both positive and negative repercussions. I tell you about both the positives and the negatives in the upcoming sections, and I also give you some guidance on dealing with any clique that has become a problem.

Be aware of your own actions regarding cliques. If you're a manager, you walk a fine line when it comes to the strategic and social aspects of your job. For example, if you're one of a few people at your organisation who cycle into work, make sure discussions about the ride in include those around you, not just the other cyclists. Asking what someone's experience is with the sport or limiting the conversation to a few highlights and moving on to another topic models appropriate attitudes and behaviour toward social groups and cliques.

Focusing on the positive

If you're experiencing some negative fallout from a particular group, keep in mind that cliques aren't all bad. Groups can offer a lot to each other and the organisation. Consider the following:

- ✔ **Cliques have power to get the job done.** Think of the jobs in your organisation that, on the surface, may have the least authority to make decisions about strategy or company direction. Now think about the people in those jobs and their ability to get together and effect change.

- ✔ **Cliques play an integral part in team morale.** They can create a sense of camaraderie that's difficult for even the most adept manager to replicate.

- ✔ **Cliques can create a sense of safety and inclusion for their members.** They can cultivate a multitude of positive experiences and workplace memories for employees.

- ✔ **Cliques can work across departments and accomplish just about any task.** When personal relationships transcend the company's structure, the give and take works for the benefit of the organisation.

- ✔ **Cliques offer social benefits.** Who wouldn't want to be part of a group that offers them pats on the back and social invitations and reminds them that they're a part of something bigger than themselves?

Understanding the negative

Cliques start to go wrong when their power goes unchecked. Managers often overlook or dismiss grumblings about cliques because, to them, the grumbling feels like high school antics.

But if you're interested in ensuring that everyone on your team gives his best and is motivated to work hard to achieve the objectives you've set out for the year, then it *is* in your best interest to address the social aspects of cliques and how they impact the organisation.

You know what's right for your situation, but consider intervening when

- Cliques are purposefully alienating others.
- Groups are closed to any perspectives other than their own.
- People are missing out on opportunities to expand their careers or view of the company.
- Alienation is causing employees to shut down and not perform to the best of their abilities.
- Bullying or inappropriate language and behaviours emerge.

Handling cliques

Sometimes intervening in cliques can be as simple as chatting with the group about how their behaviour may appear to others. Not every clique-related issue needs to be addressed with the group, though. And you often don't need to take the approach that 'If you don't have enough gum for everyone in the class, Peter, then no-one can have gum'.

Begrudging the relationships of others doesn't do anyone any good, and it's unrealistic to expect that every person in every department should be included in every activity. If one of your employees or colleagues comes to you to discuss how he feels left out because some of his co-workers have formed a trivia team on their own time and they talk about it during work hours, counsel him to participate in the conversation on a level that feels comfortable and sincere to him.

Finding allies

One unhappy employee can quickly become a dozen unhappy employees. When people are in conflict or disappointed with a policy or a decision, they tend to look for allies. Finding allies bolsters people's beliefs that they're 100 per cent right and adds fuel to the fire.

An unhealthy allegiance, one that has a negative impact on the workplace, can divide a workplace into factions and create a multitude of problems. Communication becomes difficult among members of different groups and an employee may feel that he needs to walk on eggshells to avoid saying or doing the wrong thing. This increased tension and mistrust creates more unhappy employees, and the cycle continues.

Even people who don't consider themselves part of any one group can become workplace casualties, growing dissatisfied with the tension in their environment and quitting or transferring to get away from it all. They become the innocent employees you lose by not addressing the problems.

Preventing the formation of negative groups in the first place is the preferred course of action. Encourage open communication and conflict resolution among all your staff. Be upfront about how you want everyone to resolve even minor disagreements among one another early on, instead of prolonging the dispute or going to others for coalition-building. Consider providing or asking for training on communication or conflict resolution as a way to demonstrate your support for early intervention.

So, what happens if an army of allies has successfully formed and you don't like the direction it's heading? One of the best ways to combat destructive groups or factions is to encourage more interaction among all your staff. Either create opportunities for everyone to interact together, or look for projects that include different combinations of employees. Encourage the formation of working relationships among different groups, teams or departments as a way for people to build relationships and different associations. Refocus the power of the group by using the tips I list in the 'Redefining power' section earlier in this chapter.

Creating inaccurate assumptions

Assumptions are a necessary part of life. When accurate, they keep you safe, save you time and, generally speaking, make your life easier.

But as useful as assumptions are, they can also get you into trouble. Not accurately processing the information in your environment or only seeing what you want to see can lead to incorrect assumptions. Acting on or perpetuating the assumptions by sharing them with others can start and escalate conflict. The following sections cover how people make assumptions and what you can do to prevent them from causing conflict.

Making assumptions in the first place

You and your colleagues view information and make predictions and assumptions to fit your previous experiences. Your assumptions are based on things you've learned from the physical environment and your previous experiences in similar situations. Factor in your emotional state at the time you make the assumption, and you have a general overview of how you and others come to certain conclusions.

History or experience also give you clues about a situation. Employees make assumptions based on the probability that something that has happened once will happen again, or that something that hasn't ever happened before won't ever occur.

Strong emotions can cloud your judgement and cause you to make quick and inaccurate assumptions. In important settings, like a private meeting with your boss, resist instant negative reactions to emotional assumptions you're making in the moment. Instead, suppress your urge to snap at your boss, and ask questions to clarify what she means by a particular statement.

Coming to selective conclusions

Be aware of how you and your team come to certain conclusions throughout your day, and encourage everyone to hold off making judgements until they can gather more information. Basing assumptions on cherry-picked information is dangerous and is a common contributor to miscommunication, misunderstandings, misinformation and, further down the line, destructive conflict.

When based on bad information or influenced by negative thoughts and emotions, assumptions can lead you down a false path. It's very common for employees to assume the worst or select only the information they want to hear and leave out the rest. If you want to believe that the CEO favours the marketing department, you'll scrutinise, file and catalogue every example that proves your point. Your assumptions aren't based on hard facts; instead, they're based on your overall opinion of how the company operates.

Asking rather than assuming

Be especially cautious when making decisions based on information that may actually be an assumption posing as fact. Combat the negative impact of inaccurate assumptions by gathering more information and asking questions. Try asking questions in an inquisitive, curious tone of voice rather than using an accusatory tone. You may discover a perfectly legitimate reason for a discrepancy or task not being completed, saving you from scolding your employee or colleague and looking a little silly. (More details on how to gather information and ask different kinds of questions is available in Chapter 8.)

After you check out a situation, decide how you'll react. Does the new information change anything for you? Maybe it doesn't and you can proceed as planned. Maybe it does and you can adjust accordingly. Being wrong isn't the end of the world, and checking out assumptions doesn't have to be difficult or tedious. Assume the best, use humour when appropriate, and give people the benefit of the doubt.

Perpetuating gossip

A work environment can be a breeding ground for gossip. Both accurate and inaccurate information gets spread around the workplace from person to person and group to group. You may have colleagues on your team who really enjoy gossip because it makes the workday more exciting. But gossip can also have devastating effects.

Gossip is usually about a person or a group of people, and it's usually not very flattering. I could start a rumour about myself, claiming that I have an IQ of 170, but it probably wouldn't go very far! Instead, rumours and gossip that spread the quickest are embarrassing, salacious and scandalous.

The effects of hearsay can be damaging on a variety of levels — an individual's self-esteem, a person's reputation with co-workers, and his comfort and confidence in doing his job can all be affected. Gossip on a larger scale can impact the cohesion of the workplace. No-one trusts a gossip, so team members may have difficulty having honest and unguarded conversations. Co-workers never know when information they share is going to be used against them. Mistrust significantly hinders how a group gets its work done.

Shut down gossip when you hear it. Don't let your colleagues spread negative and hurtful information, and encourage all employees to be respectful of their peers. No-one likes to discover that people are talking behind their back, so enforce a no-gossip rule. If you feel a co-worker just needs to vent or get something off his chest, listen respectfully, and then keep it to yourself. And absolutely, positively, never engage yourself in this unprofessional behaviour. Be better than that.

Chapter 4

Practising Self-Awareness: Understanding How You Foster Conflict

*I*f your team has a problem and you're wondering where to start, one of the first places to look for change may be with you. Without knowing it, you may be playing a part in creating or perpetuating a conflict.

This chapter outlines some of the common pitfalls you may make in your attempts to handle problems, whether the bickering is contained between two people or you think that a mutiny is about to happen. You also find proactive ways to manage a group, resolve issues firmly but creatively, and get on with the business at hand.

Micromanaging

Ask just about any employee what the number-one attribute of a 'bad boss' is, and she'll probably answer with one word: *Micromanaging*. Taking an inappropriate role in employee projects adds unnecessary friction to already stressful situations. Why? Because when an employee feels that her time has been wasted or that her work was for naught, she blames you.

While some employees may need more direction and attention, letting employees take the lead on a project means it'll become clear pretty quickly which ones just need some independence to shine and which ones still need your assistance. This approach helps you direct your attention where it's needed most while allowing the employees who need less TLC to flourish.

Consider these ideas as a way to micromanage less and empower more:

- **Instead of relentlessly asking questions, set mutually agreeable check-in points for an employee to update you on her project.** She can prepare a thorough briefing that you can reference later if you feel the need to examine a particular area of concern.

- **Instead of stressing about every detail, add value where your strengths shine.** If you're not that into fashion, don't worry about the colour of the shirts that the reps are wearing in the sales booth at the conference. Instead, offer to be a keynote speaker or simply a great cheerleader for everyone else's efforts.

- **Instead of swooping in at the last minute to criticise a detail, set a vision in the beginning of a project and trust your team to update you as necessary.** Save any comments at the end of a project for an appropriate time.

- **Instead of allowing a temporary fix to become a long-term management method, do what you have to do to put out a fire, but then consider coaching an employee into more independent roles.** Pair her up with a co-worker so she can learn by example, or mentor her yourself while you observe her progress.

- **Take a hint!** Some employees will try subtle and diplomatic ways to get you to back off. Some may even tell you straight up that you're meddling or smothering them. Listen and find other ways to add value instead of steamrolling over them.

Hovering over employees makes for an untrustworthy workplace. You take away an employee's opportunity to show that she's proficient when you micromanage. Ease the burden on yourself by spending less time perched over shoulders and more time focused on building strategies, relieving stress, coaching her for the next big job and showcasing your collective successes.

Stirring the Pot

Every person on a team isn't going to get along 100 per cent of the time with every one of her co-workers — that's a given. But you can help set the tone for workgroup relationships. Without even knowing it, you may be causing existing problems to inflate rather than settle down. At a minimum, assess to see whether you are

- ✔ Bringing up topics in public forums that you know are uncomfortable for one or more people in your group
- ✔ Pitting people against each other in what you think is friendly competition
- ✔ Asking members of your team to critique their co-workers
- ✔ Using sarcasm to make a point
- ✔ Publicly asking for updates on an already strained situation
- ✔ Using belittling or shaming language
- ✔ Allowing bad behaviours to become the norm
- ✔ Ignoring tension
- ✔ Playing favourites

Dividing rather than uniting

Every once in a while, you may feel like the scolding parent needing to separate the kids. That approach may give you a bit of a breather, but it doesn't solve the problems. Even if the corner you're sending someone to is a different department or simply another task, one of the employees involved is going to feel as if she's being punished — and now you've possibly made a situation worse than it was before you intervened. Temporarily separating a team that's in conflict gives you time to think, but putting yourself at the centre of their communication doesn't do much to meet a goal of solidarity.

Here are some not-so-obvious ways you could be dividing your team:

- ✔ **Using divisive language:** Using subtle language like 'they' and 'them' is a way of dividing a team. An employee is more apt to feel ownership in a solution if you use words like 'us' and 'we' and work to unite the sides instead of playing into any perceived or real separations.

- ✔ **Holding exhaustive general brainstorming sessions and staff meetings:** In your endeavour to include everyone in the decision-making process, you take it a little too far and spend too long in the idea-generating phase. Then people start taking sides and the dynamics of the meeting change. One person gives up the debate and shuts down, another pulls out the soapbox and demands that the others see it her way, and before you know it you've created an underlying animosity in the group that didn't exist before your attempt to 'pull everyone together'. (For tips on how to manage the brainstorming process, check out Chapter 10.)

- ✔ **Making concessions for an employee:** Granting one-off concessions to one employee can lead to that employee being shunned by colleagues, other employees asking for their own exceptions, and you unintentionally setting a precedent that every decision is going to be up for a group vote.

- ✔ **Creating a false sense of security:** Even the most skilled listener can unwittingly create a feeling of betrayal in a staff member. Keep up the active listening skills, but be sure you're not just telling everyone what they want to hear. Set accurate expectations, coach employees through behaviours that may be contributing to conflicts, and be specific about how, why and with whom you'll follow up.

Appearing to take sides

You may wonder how you're not supposed to take sides when the higher-ups are looking to you to manage situations on your team. You should be able to make decisions, but how you go about making them matters to employees. You need to listen to all sides, ask pertinent questions, fully understand the situation, and *then* make a decision.

Assuming that the sales team is always right or that the apprentice has no place having a different perspective than the expert mechanic may get you into trouble. If you manage a team, you're everyone's manager — not the manager of just a select few. You may take a lot of pride in your mentoring skills, but choosing just one or two of your staff members to groom could backfire by causing the other team members to turn against your protégé.

Instead of showing favouritism, demonstrate that you're equally interested in everyone's career and growth path by looking for opportunities to further individual education or experience levels.

Not Taking the Time to Gain Understanding

Busy, busy, busy. When you have your head down in the books or when you're barrelling along to meet an important deadline, you may cause ripples in the pond without even knowing you threw the pebble! Not slowing down long enough to understand the broader picture or focus your attention in the other direction short-changes your staff and weakens your reputation.

Overreacting

How you present situations to your team affects their reactions. If you're always fired up, your crew will likely follow suit. A hyper-emotional approach to problems cultivates the feeling that no-one has an eye on finding solutions. Keep day-to-day reactions below a simmer, so when things do get tough, your employees don't boil over. You set the example, and your team is looking to you for direction.

Misunderstanding the real issues

Looking at the surface issues of disagreements and ignoring the underlying values and emotions at play means you're missing an opportunity to find better, more durable solutions to problems. You can accomplish a lot more if you know how to read between the lines and capture what's most important for your employees. It may take some time and a little research to really get to the root of the problem, but it'll be worth it when you're able to help employees resolve the real issues. Assessing a problem can be tricky, so see Chapter 5 for some assistance. Chapter 2 can help you figure out what makes employees tick and Chapters 6 through 9 cover the steps for holding a successful mediation.

Looking the other way

You may be tempted to ignore a problem when you don't know what you can do to stop behaviours that adversely affect your team. But overlooking signs of unrest erodes your authority and your reputation. Watch for the following:

- **Bullying:** Bullying is one of the most obvious yet commonly overlooked behaviours. It can be subtle or overt, and you may find yourself ignoring it because, well, you're a bit intimidated by the bully yourself. Badgering and baiting is never acceptable, so gather whatever resources you need to address the situation, but handle it nonetheless.

- **Power struggles:** Playing tug of war is a fun activity at the company picnic, but it has no place on a functional team. If a staff member is trying to one-up a colleague, is putting a team member down to build herself up, or is lobbying against her co-workers, check out what may really be happening with that person. If it makes sense for the personalities involved, consider strengthening the weakest link rather than taking away from the strongest. (For more tips on understanding power issues, check out Chapter 3.)

Less obvious but perhaps just as frustrating for your staff is when you ignore their requests for your time. Sure, you're busy, but being available only via email or agreeing to meetings and then not showing up is disrespectful to your crew. Scheduling, and keeping, face-to-face time is essential. And when you do meet with an employee, move away from the computer and turn off your mobile phone — she'll appreciate the attention.

Being dismissive

If someone has the courage to talk to you about an issue, pay attention. Disregarding emotions or anxiety an employee feels about a situation with her co-workers (including you) may cause her to skip coming to you next time. Instead, she may go behind your back, go over your head, stew or adversely affect the company by carrying out negative actions.

Here are some ways in which you may be dismissing an employee:

- ✔ **Telling her it's her imagination, that she's being hypersensitive or even that she's exaggerating.** Instead, ask good questions, do a little investigating, and coach her to handle it herself (see Chapter 5 for tips on empowering your employees). Be sure to check back in with her to see how it's going.

- ✔ **Defending or speaking for the other person.** It's okay to offer a bit of conjecture as you ask her why she thinks her co-worker may be doing what he's doing, but taking on the role of defender won't sit well with the confider.

- ✔ **Saying, 'Let's get back to some real work, okay?'** Dismissing her distress, even if you have listened to her outline her problems, not only keeps a conflict brewing, but also adds you to the list of individuals she's upset with. Choosing between a task and a person isn't necessary. You can do both by hearing out an employee and by working with her to solve her problems — so she can get back to work.

- ✔ **Making a commitment to look into concerns and then not following through in a meaningful way.** You may wholeheartedly believe that what an employee is telling you is true and, with the best of intentions, promise to take care of the problem. However, if you take too long to address the issue, try to cure the symptom rather than the disease, or simply muff up the whole situation, the employee may interpret your actions as a way to dismiss her and her concerns.

- ✔ **Limiting what you think an employee can contribute.** Dismissing an employee's or colleague's offers of help or requests for more responsibility will likely annoy them and create resentments and tension.

Talking about the Work Ineffectively

How you discuss what you're doing, what your staff are up to and what's happening on a daily basis really matters to your team. If employees feel you have their backs, they're more likely to watch out for one another and demonstrate their loyalty to you.

The more informed your team is, the less likely they are to fill in the blanks with erroneous or hurtful information.

Not sharing your contributions

Though most employees complain about micromanagers (refer to the earlier section 'Micromanaging'), your staff most likely want you to show them you're doing *something*. Simply saying, 'Wow, I can't believe how busy I am!' probably isn't enough. You don't need to share every detail from your calendar or spend hours going over your business plans for the year, but letting an employee know what you're doing and why you're headed in a particular direction makes it easier for her to have your back with others in the company and may keep her from badmouthing you as a manager.

Instead of trying to fly under the radar, try

- **Creating easy ways to update the group.** Staff meetings, conference calls or emails go a long way toward getting the team up to date on what everyone is doing. Include yourself in any update conversations.

- **Doing what you say you're going to do.** If you assign yourself a task, do it. Taking responsibility for a job and then having someone else do the work erodes your integrity. If you know you don't have the time, energy or skill set to complete a task, set expectations from the start.

- **Explaining yourself.** If you leave your employees in the dark, they'll find ways to assume you're doing nothing.

Underrepresenting your team

Spending more time schmoozing with the top dog than working with your crew in the trenches makes it hard for employees to believe you're in tune with their career needs. Even when you have the best of intentions and all you're trying to do is make sure your team is recognised, the appearance of catering and pandering to the powers that be can damage your reputation back on the shop floor. The only thing your staff see is you distancing yourself from them, which leads them to think you're only in it for yourself.

To combat a self-serving perception, present your hard work as team-focused. Your employees will probably appreciate your efforts to lobby for additional funds or your endeavours to get them new resources. What they won't appreciate are overt actions that appear only to benefit you. People know the difference between the two approaches, and their reactions to you will be 180 degrees different. Working on their behalf and being a trusted representative of their concerns wins you loyalty.

Conversely, you may have a strained or difficult relationship with upper management that frustrates your employees. You can easily think negatively about the higher-ups when they make decisions you don't agree with, especially if it involves an ongoing issue. When continually fighting with the execs is the rule not the exception, you run the risk of alienating yourself and your team from the main decision-makers.

Regardless of your approach with upper management, when an employee feels that you don't have her back, she takes steps to protect herself. Her dissatisfaction most likely won't begin and end with you. She'll do what she feels she needs to do to step over others, deftly move around you and capture whatever spotlight she can whenever she can. Elevators, lunch lines and car parks are great places for her to talk to upper management herself!

If you place employees in the predicament of having to fight for attention, they fight among themselves. Avoid an employees-versus-management mentality by being the bridge between the two. Make sure your staff know that you're working the company hierarchy for everyone's benefit, not just your own, and work to improve any strained relationships with executives.

Creating Ill-Defined Expectations and Responsibilities

You're probably already aware that not having detailed job descriptions is an obvious cause for concern among employees. But what may be less obvious are the directives you give on a daily basis that also have the potential to cause problems between your employees, such as:

 ✔ **Using hazy terms to give what you consider to be clear instructions.** Telling an employee 'This is a priority' sounds pretty clear, but what's missing in that directive is a description of what this is a priority over. One person may construe your order to mean that he should drop everything and concentrate on the task. Another team member may take it to mean that she should make time for the priority task but continue with her other responsibilities, too. If he stops what he's doing and she doesn't, she may be upset that he's stopped working on what she needs, and he may be upset that she's not giving the task enough attention.

✔ **Assigning a task or responsibility to more than one person.** Assigning a task to more than one person almost always causes tension between those people. You may feel you're just sharing your new ideas, but if you're not clear on how these ideas are going to be actioned, and by whom, you can cause duplication and anger and, ultimately, conflict.

✔ **Couching language because you're worried an employee may not react well to an instruction.** The people who work for you are pretty smart cookies, and if you're less than honest about your expectations, they'll soon figure it out. If you sugar-coat the fact that you need an employee to work overtime when you say, 'Run those numbers when you can', she won't be too happy when she learns from someone else that you need the report for an 8 am meeting tomorrow.

✔ **Making promises or setting expectations with vendors, customers or people from other areas of the company, and then expecting your staff to deliver disappointing news.** Putting employees' professional reputations at stake is always a bad move. If you've mistakenly set an unrealistic expectation, cowboy up and admit the error to the outsider instead of ordering your employees to do it for you. If you had time to make the promise in the first place, you have time to adjust expectations.

✔ **Setting expectations that are beyond what an employee can accomplish.** Setting unrealistic expectations can cause your employee to have low self-esteem and feel overwhelmed and stressed, which, in turn, may lead her to give up, quit or talk trash about her situation. Brainstorm with her about what you can do to ease the burden — and set more realistic expectations in the future.

✔ **Employing a military-type approach that includes barking orders at subordinates.** On the surface, this approach may seem to be the most efficient way to get a clear and concise message out to the troops. But if you're leaving out important parts of the instructions (like the strategy behind them!), you run the risk of creating infighting while team members stumble into each other in their panic to react. It only takes a few more seconds to share with employees your strategy or thought process when you're handing out assignments.

Hiring the Right Person for the Wrong Job

Exemplary individual contributors commonly get attention and gain respect from management. You may have a staff member who does a bang-up job with every assignment you've ever given her. Perhaps the two of you have even developed a mentor–student relationship and you're ready to move her to the next step in her career. The only problem: You may be setting her, and the rest of the team, up for a conflict if you move her into a new role without first giving her the tools she needs to succeed.

Hiring someone from the outside or allowing an internal lateral move can be just as tricky as promotions. Even though a person has received high marks for her work in one area, you can't assume that her skills will easily translate into another role. Any time a change occurs, it affects everyone — and not planning ahead can lead to an uproar.

Here's how to prepare everyone for personnel changes:

- ✔ **Thoroughly discuss with an employee her strengths and areas for improvement.** Build a plan to baby-step her into the new role before she takes the job. Consider training for certain job functions or additional people skills. Take the time to groom and prepare her for the next steps.

- ✔ **Ask other employees to share confidentially how they see a potential employee's skill set.** What's her reputation in the industry? Where could she improve? Some of the answers you get may be the result of the employee wanting to be politically correct; others may be the result of jealousy and resistance to change. Use your best judgement to sift through the information and listen to the team. You may learn something!

- ✔ **Test the waters.** If you're planning to promote a team member from an individual contributor to a supervisory position, consider creating situations that allow everyone on the team to try out bits of the change a little at a time. Can you form a committee or task force, putting the employee at the helm, to see how she does in the new role? Maybe putting her in charge for an interim period of time — say, while you're on holiday — will give all parties an opportunity to get used to the idea and bring any potential pitfalls to the surface. Think in terms of milestones rather than sweeping changes all at once.

✔ **Lessen the impact of the change.** Be open with the team about the change and discuss how it will benefit them. Will the change ease the communication process, lighten workloads or make for shorter days? What's in it for the team if an employee is promoted or newly hired?

Living in Fix-It Mode

Moving projects forward, meeting deadlines and getting some tangible results under your belt are all seemingly reasonable justifications for fixing a mess yourself instead of putting the onus for solutions on employees.

Additionally, being a good listener, mentoring employees and fully investigating the source of problems takes time. When there's a tonne of work to be done, time is of the essence and you may have developed a few survival tactics — but these may be causing strife among your employees. Avoid the following approaches to solving issues because they could be giving you more — not less — to do.

Talking instead of listening

Who likes to listen to long-winded lectures and dry-as-dirt sermons? You probably don't, so why assume any of your colleagues like it. If you're guilty of pulling out a soapbox and spouting your view before fully investigating a conflict, consider a change.

Even though you're expected to handle flare-ups as they arise, be sure you really listen to what your employees are saying before you make decisions that don't consider their needs. If your only focus is on telling your team what you want to see rather than listening to what's happening, you miss out on key information and opportunities to improve the overall work environment. Your team is in the trenches every day, and they know what's getting in the way of good business or causing conflicts to recycle. Asking questions to understand gives you a better view of what's happening, so you can implement a strategy that reduces future conflict and increases productivity.

And, while you're at it, fake listening isn't a good idea either. Don't spend time asking your employees what they'd like to see happen or what ideas they have for viable solutions (making them feel as if they're part of a remedy) if you've already decided what's going to happen. You'll add another layer to the conflict — even if you have the best of intentions.

Being judge and jury

Jump into a sticky situation, make a few quick decisions and everything's fixed, right? The problem with that is that not only are you most likely missing some of the key elements of the dispute, but you're also placing yourself at the centre of every difference of opinion.

Being the judge and jury inadvertently creates a dependence on you as the only decision-maker in the group. Over time, employees either resent you for not letting them be involved in solving their own problems or become completely paralysed when faced with a decision.

Work with individuals to come up with their own answers. People are capable of solving their own problems — sometimes they just need some assistance. Be a sounding-board by listening to your employees' concerns and then ask questions to help them consider options. Questions like the ones in Chapter 8 help your staff get to the heart of a dispute and find satisfying solutions.

Rescuing instead of coaching

Occasionally, an employee in the centre of a conflict may tug at your heartstrings. Taking on the role of caregiver every once in a while isn't unusual, but feeling sorry for or empathetic toward an employee's social awkwardness or lack of training keeps a conflict going. Telling her co-workers to overlook her need for development short-changes everyone and doesn't solve anything; it can actually make the situation worse, by creating resentment in the employees who end up doing more and limiting the potential of the person you're trying to rescue.

An employee who wants and expects you to fix the situation for her may actually end up resenting you. She may even get angry when you tell her that you won't do for her what she can do for herself. Plus, you run the risk that you'll be put in a bad spot if things don't go well. The very person you're trying to help can easily turn on you if she doesn't get what she wants.

Coach and empower an employee to handle situations herself so that she gains the necessary skills to handle future situations better, improve her working relationships, and expand the skills that lead to less conflict overall. Help her identify the problem areas and brainstorm ways she can be more independent.

Always putting yourself in the role of the lifeguard makes for some pretty weak swimmers! If you've created a team of dependent employees, it's not too late to strengthen the aptitude for problem-solving you already have. Use the skills in this book to mediate conflicts, arrange group meetings in which the team finds their own solutions, and reach out to others to find the resources your team needs.

Denying Shortfalls

Owning up to the possibility that you may not have every skill or quality it takes to be a perfect manager is tough. I won't ask you to reveal all your shortcomings to your team, but I will ask that, when you make a mistake, you're humble enough to admit that you were wrong. If you don't have all the information, be willing to ask for help. Admitting that you made a mistake or need assistance makes you human. It also allows your team to show its strength and feel closer by supporting you when you need it. Demonstrate your willingness to be vulnerable, and your staff will be more likely to admit their own shortfalls instead of going to great lengths to cover them up.

Letting egos get in the way

Taking credit for work you had little or no part in, dismissing the efforts of employees, or clamouring to get your name mentioned before those on your team is not only egotistical but also turns the very people who are there to support you against you. Be a cheerleader for your team, and they'll return the favour. Pushing a boulder uphill with all hands on deck is easier than going it alone.

Pulling rank is your prerogative and, yes, sometimes it's necessary. Play the boss card when you feel that doing so is absolutely essential. Your team knows you're the manager — you don't have to remind them daily. They'll appreciate you *showing* them you're the manager rather than telling them. Use motivating language such as 'I know you have what it takes to do the job' instead of 'Because I'm the boss — that's why!'

Lacking training or skills

Every once in a while, you'll come up against a situation that tests your knowledge and capabilities. Maybe it's that one employee who doesn't respond to your usual approaches or techniques. Or maybe your boss is pushing for more than you can deliver and you're simply out of your element.

Knowing that you should do something but not getting the help you need to pull it off can get you in trouble. Instead, you're likely to get much better results if you listen to a mentor or the human resources (HR) department for possible solutions.

Being uncomfortable with change

If you're a manager who doesn't do well with change and you're stuck in the middle of one, you may resort to

- ✔ **Hiding:** If you're not available, employees have to deal with the stress and confusion on their own. Leaving your employees to fend for themselves breeds discontent. It goes without saying, then, that you have to show up and have a calm, consistent presence in the face of change.

- ✔ **Fighting:** If you're uncomfortable or unhappy with changes that are occurring, you may decide to fight the new world order with everything you've got, and lose sight of the big picture.

  Yes, fighting for what you believe in is important, but don't forget to take a break once in a while and reassess the situation. Remind yourself of your ultimate goal, and keep your employees' interests in mind at all times. As the situation evolves, you don't want to find yourself so caught up in 'winning' that you miss a key opportunity for positive change.

- ✔ **Surrendering:** Often, accepting the inevitable makes sense, and finding ways to communicate the benefits of a change helps your employees work through disappointing decisions. But if your team is willing to come up with viable alternatives to a decision, and you just want to give up, their morale can be seriously affected and you could be setting the stage for irreparable harm.

✔ A period of change is not the time to inadvertently bring your team together against you or sit on the sidelines as people get their résumés in order. Instead, put your energy to good use and help the group formulate a cohesive response that takes all sides into account. If the ideas are shot down and the group receives a clear 'no', at least they can move on _with_ you rather than _against_ you.

Chapter 5

Knowing When to Address Conflict

*M*anagers often overlook the cost of conflict, or the cost of doing nothing about a conflict, when considering the impact of disagreements. It may not always feel like it, but resolving conflict at the lowest level possible saves you time, money and energy.

This chapter provides insight into whether you should step in to mediate a conflict on your team. It also gives you ways to monitor progress if you decide to put the resolution process in the hands of the employees involved.

Assessing the Cost and Severity of the Conflict

Sometimes giving a conflict time to work out on its own is worthwhile, but you won't know whether you're doing the right thing without investigating to see whether your strategy has an impact on your teams' productivity and the bottom line. Taking a broad view of the situation and considering both hard costs (like lost inventory) and soft costs (like team morale) helps you determine whether it's time to step in.

Hard costs associated with unresolved conflict

Hard costs are measurable costs that can be deducted from your financial statements. These are items like lost inventory, legal fees and revenue decreases from lost sales. Though they're tangible and usually easy to find and add up, people often overlook them in the midst of conflict. Here are some of the more common hard costs that could be attributed to unresolved conflict:

- **Wasted time:** Time is money, and people avoiding one another and delaying outcomes creates a cost. People in conflict have to have an outlet for their emotions and can often waste time by commiserating with anyone who will listen as a way to vent what's happening. Employees start avoiding one another, taking longer lunches and breaks, and coming in late or leaving early as a way to cope.

  Pay attention to the number of hours being wasted in a day or week and consider whether you can afford to wait this out.

- **Lost workdays/absenteeism:** When people are uneasy in an environment, they seek the comfort of home. If you're expecting people who are in conflict (or who are surrounded by conflict) to work without resolution, they may be taking sick days just to avoid the stress.

- **Reduced productivity:** People often find their thoughts drifting to a conflict and replaying it over and over, thinking about what went wrong, why they're right and then snapping back to reality when the phone rings. You're probably spending precious work time thinking about the situation, too — and you may not even be one of the people directly involved! When you have to work on a project with someone you're not getting along with, the job takes longer and the final product is affected.

- **Performance and quality:** Even if you don't see a marked drop in productivity, you'll probably notice a diminished quality in the work that's being delivered. Someone has to pick up the slack and correct mistakes that are made due to other distractions, and that someone may be you.

  Distractions get in the way of an individual's ability to be creative, and the company may be losing out on good ideas and clever solutions to problems.

✔ **Sabotage and theft:** If employees reach a point where they feel no-one cares about a situation, sabotage and theft isn't that unusual. Sabotage or theft can be as simple as an employee removing or hiding inventory or equipment, or as underhanded as taking ideas to another company where the employee will be rewarded and not looked at as the person with the problem.

✔ **Turnover:** Regardless of the size of your organisation, a dollar amount is associated with the cost of hiring, processing and training every new employee.

✔ **Termination packages:** If your human resources (HR) department determines that a conflict carries a potential legal risk to the company — for example, it involves bullying or discrimination — HR may negotiate a termination package that includes additional financial remuneration.

✔ **Legal costs:** How far an employee is willing to take a conflict to prove a point, to get you or a colleague once and for all, or simply to buy himself some time while he considers other career options is often unpredictable. Cases that can create high legal costs usually arise from conflicts that involve bullying, discrimination or workers compensation. After a lawsuit is filed, your organisation will spend money on legal fees and wages for all the employees who are addressing the court case, not to mention that this money isn't going toward productivity or more sales.

Soft costs associated with unresolved conflict

Soft costs, on the surface, are those things that may not seem measurable or easily assigned a specific dollar amount, but they still affect your bottom line. Soft costs often distinguish you from your competitors — they're the intangibles that contribute to or detract from your success. Here are just a few examples of soft costs:

✔ **Morale:** People are likely aware of an ongoing conflict, and this awareness can affect morale on all levels. Even staff who aren't directly involved in the conflict may start to believe that the company doesn't care, and so start to question why they should give it their all.

✔ **Decreased customer service:** If someone who deals with clients is unhappy, you run the risk of her taking it out, knowingly or not, on customers. The cost on the bottom line could be devastating.

✔ **Reputation:** Word gets around fast when people find a great enterprise that really values its employees. When conflict goes unresolved, it also affects a company's reputation. Disgruntled employees' comments can scare off a future valued employee and potential customers.

✔ **Loss of skilled employees:** In addition to the hard costs associated with employee turnover, consider the soft costs when a skilled employee leaves out of frustration, takes with him everything you taught him, and gives his expertise to your competitors. And you have to retrain a new hire.

Determining severity

A problem between employees is severe when it costs you more to ignore than it does to address it. If an employee has placed a letter of resignation on your desk or if important documents have come up missing, for example, the problem has moved from a minor disagreement to a severe conflict.

Use the lists in the sections in this chapter to help you determine whether the few people involved can work things out on their own or can manage to get beyond the problem with a little coaching from you. If minimal intervention doesn't resolve the problem, it's severe enough to require a mediation meeting like the one I outline in Chapters 6 to 9.

Approaching Employees and Gathering Information

If you've determined that the cost of doing nothing about a conflict is too high, it's time to take action and address the issue. Tactfully approach those impacted and see if you can get at what's really going on.

Knowing your intent

Before you begin any conversations with your colleagues, know what your intention for meeting is. Will you call them in for a disciplinary action, or will you have a discussion that encourages them to be a part of the solution? Determine whether you're on a fact-finding mission and going to HR for documentation, or you're going to allow room for a confidential conversation.

Try to resolve the conflict at the lowest possible level. Plan a resolution strategy that uses the least amount of escalation. Start with the colleagues involved before you bring in anyone else. Your intention should be for those involved to save face, for them to see that they can work out disagreements on their own, and for you to keep the cost (and exposure) of the conflict down. Let your colleagues feel empowered by their ability to work things out rather than afraid of what may show up in their personnel files.

Although your intention may be to act as an objective facilitator, tell the employees upfront what your organisation requires you to report so they can determine for themselves what they're comfortable sharing with you.

Sorting out the players

Create a list for yourself that includes those directly involved in the conflict, and then add any other staff members who may be affected by the problem. If you learn from your initial conversations that another person needs to be involved, you can easily add her to a mediated conversation.

As you meet with each person, ask whom they see as key players in resolving the conflict. If it becomes apparent that a number of people are involved and their presence in a meeting is necessary to reach a resolution, look to Chapter 10 for processes to facilitate larger meetings.

When employees are in conflict, they often build armies as a means to strengthen their point of view. Make sure to check in with secondary players to determine their level of involvement and whether you think they'll be valuable in resolving the issue. They may be satisfied just knowing that the conflict is being addressed and learning about the outcomes at a later date. You don't need to involve the whole gang if you can resolve the conflict with just a few people.

Considering the meeting place

Where you meet communicates a lot to other colleagues. If everyone sees one closed-door meeting after another, fear and stress can escalate. Your colleagues will be more focused on what's happening behind the door than on their work. Similarly, publicly walking up to someone's cubicle and starting a conversation where others can overhear can cause your staff to shut down and share very little, causing you to miss important information.

Consider what's commonplace for you and the least disruptive for those involved. If it's not out of the norm for you to ask someone to stick around after a meeting, do that. If it's going to raise concerns and curiosity, think twice. Whatever you decide, your goal should be to choose a place that is private and inconspicuous, where people can speak freely.

Being consistent in your inquiries

When you begin approaching employees to gather information, be consistent with all parties. Prepare a simple statement that explains the approach you're taking to resolve the matter. I like to use language as simple as the following:

> I'd like to talk with you about your working relationship with Ted. I'm going to be talking to him as well to get his perspective. My intention is to understand each of your perspectives, and I hope we can resolve this ourselves. I won't be sharing anything you tell me with Ted or anyone else. Can you share with me what's been happening for you?

End the discussion by letting both parties know what type of follow-up you've planned, even if it's just to give the situation more thought. Give them time to consider how they want to proceed and let them know when you'll be checking back in with them. Also provide a way for them to correspond privately with you.

Asking questions

Keeping the questions open ended rather than asking questions that only require a yes or a no draws out more information. Open-ended inquiries allow your employees to tell their stories while you get beyond the surface details you may already know.

Here are some of my favourite questions to get you started:

- ✔ What's been happening for you in this situation?
- ✔ What have you tried to do to resolve the conflict?
- ✔ What do you think the next steps are to resolve this situation?
- ✔ Who do you believe needs to be involved to resolve it?
- ✔ Can I offer you any additional support?

Evaluating the Details of the Conflict

If the conflict in your workplace involves a threat to safety or a glaring legal issue, deal with it immediately. Beyond an emergency situation, put the pieces of the story together to determine whether you need to intervene.

What you know

After your individual conversations with the main players and those employees affected by the conflict (refer to the earlier section 'Approaching Employees and Gathering Information'), you should have a pretty good idea about what's been going on. You can probably even see that those involved may have had the best of intentions, but a miscommunication has kept them from seeing each other's perspective and moving past the problem.

You should also have a clear idea of the timeline of events. This conflict may have started at different times for different people. The individuals involved may not even be upset by the same incidents! When you know who the key players are, how long things have been brewing and who needs to participate in creating solutions, consider what you've observed in the working environment. These are the kinds of things you've probably noticed but haven't thought to add to the list. They're important, so pay attention to

- ✔ Reactions from team members when those in conflict interact.
- ✔ Contradictions in the stories being told by those involved.

- ✔ Body language, such as rolling eyes, avoiding eye contact, not acknowledging one another and just plain tension in the room.

- ✔ Expressed (or overheard) frustration from other team members.

- ✔ Resistance to working on group projects.

Don't be surprised if, at this point, you feel you can solve the problem in record time. All you have to do is call everyone together and announce your decision. Problem solved, move on. But wait! If you take full responsibility for deciding the outcome this time, you're setting a precedent for future conflicts and not giving staff a chance to fully understand the problems and feel empowered to avoid them in the future.

Instead, follow these recommendations based on your unique situation:

- ✔ **If you know that both employees see a problem and express an interest in finding an answer,** allow them to try to resolve the conflict on their own (see the section 'Empowering Employees to Handle the Issue Themselves'). You can still step in to mediate later if necessary.

- ✔ **If you know that one employee acknowledges a problem but the other doesn't,** help the employee who's denying the difficulty to see the benefits of having a conversation with the other person. They could have a productive conversation on their own, or you may need to mediate their meeting. (For guidance on facilitating a meeting, see Chapters 6 to 9.)

- ✔ **If you know that neither party believes there's a problem,** you need to consider a course of action that takes into account the impact that the conflict is having on the rest of the team and what it's costing the company. If the impact and cost is minimal, you can give it some time. If you're not comfortable with the level of impact, act by either mediating a meeting between the two parties (see Chapters 6 through 9) or begin planning for a team meeting (see Chapter 10).

- ✔ **If you know that a conflict is affecting your entire team,** use techniques customised to resolve group conflict effectively. (Chapter 10 provides a detailed process you can use.)

Follow-up conversations

If the problem isn't affecting the whole team, give the parties
a little time to figure things out on their own. Even if you learn
that one or both employees seemed oblivious to the conflict, the
fact that you had initial conversations will highlight the need for
them to do *something*. Allow time for them to connect to resolve
the issues, and then schedule individual follow-up conversations.
Here are some questions to ask at the meetings:

- How have things been since we last met?

- Do you feel the situation is improving?

- What have you tried?

- What do you need to do to move forward from here?

- Would you be willing to meet with the other person if
  necessary?

Empowering Employees to Handle the Issue Themselves

People commonly want to save face and try to resolve a problem
without their manager's involvement. So, if those involved all
feel confident they can handle the situation on their own, let
them work it out.

Even though you aren't guiding them through the conflict
resolution process, you can help colleagues prepare for the
conversations that they'll have with each other. Communicate
your expectations for follow-through clearly, and include
housekeeping details and information regarding decisions such
as the following:

- Whether their communication will be part of their
  personnel files.

- Confidentiality — indicate who needs to know about the
  meeting and agreements.

- The timeframe in which you expect them to meet.

- Your availability for the meeting if needed and how they'll
  let you know.

- What type of feedback you'll need from their meeting (written or verbal).

- How they plan to address future disagreements.

- How often and in what format you'd like to be informed about progress.

- The exact date you'll be checking back in with them.

- When and where they'll meet (think safety, comfort and time of day).

- Resources they may need from you, such as access to a private meeting room or someone to cover their shifts.

- Whether agreements will be in writing or a handshake will do, as well as the level of detail needed in an agreement (such as a summary for you but a detailed document for them).

- What they'll do if they come to a standstill.

- What homework or preparation is needed prior to the meeting so they have important information on hand.

Providing tips for success

Let both parties know you're rooting for them, that you have confidence in their ability to look at the situation from each other's point of view, and that you're ready to help them as needed.

Coach the parties at various points in the process by doing the following:

- **Ask them to treat each other with common courtesy and to walk away from the conversation without doing additional damage to each other.** Being your best can be difficult when you disagree with someone. Frustration can set in, and you can find yourself responding defensively. Get a firm commitment from both employees that if either person becomes frustrated to the point that he wants to verbally attack the other person and the conversation goes south, one of them will ask for a break and the other will honour the request when asked. A walk around the block may give them enough time to cool off before continuing.

- **Ask them to listen, and assure them that listening doesn't mean agreeing with what the other person is saying.** Listening demonstrates that you respect the other person enough to hear what's important to her. Ask them not to interrupt one another, and encourage note taking when the urge to say something out of turn arises. Discuss the importance of restating what they heard the other say as a way to demonstrate a willingness to begin to see the other person's perspective.

✓ **Encourage sharing.** In one-on-one conversations, you may have heard some key information that, if it were shared, would help create understanding and move the parties forward. When one person doesn't see things the same as someone else does, he'll often hold back information. People do this out of fear of being ridiculed for their point of view or so they can use it against the other person later if needed. Let both employees know that sharing certain details would help everyone make the best decision and move forward. Simply say something like, 'I don't think she's aware of that and if I was talking with you and you shared that with me, it would change my view of things.'

Motivating your employees to succeed

People are more motivated to put their energy into something when they can see the benefit in trying. Help both parties see that they're in the driver's seats here. They have the opportunity to tell each other what's important and to ask for what they need. They'll be more likely to follow the solutions if they reach them together than they would if they had to carry out a mandate handed down from someone else.

If they need you or someone else to make a decision, they can always ask for that, but let them know now's the time to try it on their own first.

You may be tempted to encourage them to focus on resolution as the primary motivation to put this conflict behind them and be done with it. Unfortunately, that approach can put pressure on them to find an answer — any answer — even if it's not something that'll work. Let them know their time will be well spent if they come away understanding what's most important to the other person, and that you're not interested in a quick fix. Assure them that you have other resources available to help them if needed.

Wrapping it up

No matter the outcome of their discussion, they'll want to know what to do next and how to end a meeting. They'll need to discuss and share the logistics of their next steps. Let them know that you'll expect some sort of feedback, even if the information they share is that they're giving it more thought.

If they come up with a number of steps that they need to carry out in order to resolve the conflict, make sure they've taken the time to consider the order and timeline of the steps — the how and when. Have them put their agreement in writing — this strategy can prevent future conflicts if one person forgets an important step.

Finally, tell them that you'll expect them to consider the future. How do they want to approach one another if either person feels a need to meet? Have the parties consider how they'll follow up with you and how they intend to meet the expectations you gave them from the 'Empowering Employees to Handle the Issue Themselves' section earlier in this chapter.

Watching Their Progress

Your colleagues have met and all seems well after their conversation. You're hopeful that the conflict is behind them and that they're both moving on. So how will you know if things are on track or if you need to step in with another course of action? You have to pay attention to determine what's next.

Complimenting their progress

Give your employees a little recognition for the risks they took in trying to resolve a conflict themselves; they'll appreciate it even if they were unsuccessful in resolving the situation. Say something like, 'I appreciate your willingness to give it a shot. It's not always easy to see eye to eye on things. Your willingness to try indicates to me that we'll find an answer. We may just need to try a different approach.'

Keep in mind each person's comfort level with receiving compliments — some people are a bit uncomfortable with praise. Even if one of your team members is the most humble person around, you can find a way to compliment him. A sincere email, handwritten note, or after-hours voicemail can go a long way in helping him know he's on the right track.

Knowing what to watch for

Look for a number of different, sometimes subtle, indicators to determine whether your employees have been successful in putting the past behind them. Your answers to the following questions can help you pinpoint trouble spots:

- ✔ How do they interact? Are they respectful of one another? Are the other team members comfortable with how the two are behaving?
- ✔ Are they able to share information freely?
- ✔ Can they work together when necessary?
- ✔ Are they finishing projects in a timely manner?
- ✔ Are they working through problems or pointing fingers?
- ✔ Do repeat issues keep popping up?

Responding to progress

Keep a watchful but restrained eye on the situation. If you overdo it, your questions will remind them of their troubles and may indicate that you don't trust them to follow through.

If you think that they're doing really well, you can casually say, 'How's it been going since you talked?' and give them space to share their good news. If you see specific concerns, bring those to light and ask for any solutions. You may say, 'I noticed whenever we have a new contract come up that the two of you seem a bit tense. Can we do anything to prevent that?'

 Your check-ins should be matched appropriately to specific, observable behaviour. Not checking in at all could lead them to feel unsupported and uncomfortable asking for additional resources that they feel are necessary for continued success.

Chapter 6

Developing a Plan and Preparing for a Meeting

· ·

In This Chapter

▶ Informing employees about the meeting

▶ Setting boundaries and expectations

▶ Creating an inviting meeting space

▶ Preparing to facilitate

· ·

*M*anagers often have to address the conflicts of the people on their team, and some try to rush headlong into a conversation with the people in conflict, without giving much thought to the process or the techniques that could maximise their chances of success. But this approach doesn't usually yield good long-term results.

Solving your employees' conflicts for them actually does more harm than good. Employees are more likely to support an idea when they have a stake in creating the solution than when someone else arbitrarily decides the answer for them. After all, they're the ones who have to live with the consequences.

This line of thinking may represent a dramatic shift for you, but don't worry — I fill you in on a proven process that not only solves problems but also strengthens people's ability to tackle future issues.

This chapter is dedicated to all the initial work you can do to prepare your employees or colleagues for a productive conflict resolution meeting. In this type of mediation, you facilitate discussion only — the responsibility for creative solutions and decisions ultimately will rest on the shoulders of the folks who are in conflict.

Preparing the Parties for a Conversation

If your employees have reached the point where they need some help, it's time to intervene and facilitate a mediated conversation. (Refer to Chapter 5 for information on knowing when to address conflict.) Follow this strategic process that takes your employees from preparing, to sharing, to understanding, to brainstorming, to agreement. I give you all the preparation details you need in this section; Chapters 7, 8, and 9 help you work through the remaining stages of the process.

In the upcoming sections, I cover the elements of a good preparatory approach. I break them out and discuss each in detail, but you should include them in one succinct email or conversation.

Inviting your employees to the meeting

Every meeting starts with an invitation, and mediation is no different. This step of your strategic process can vary, depending on the relationship you have with the parties involved, the kind of workplace you're in and the policies surrounding dispute resolution. I outline two good invitation options in the upcoming sections.

Regardless of how you opt to let the parties know it's time to talk, the goal of the invitation is to

- ✔ Share information about the process
- ✔ Allow the parties to voice any initial concerns
- ✔ Prepare them to share their perspective at the meeting

The timing of this invitation may be as important as the invitation itself. Whether you choose to inform your employees that you're requesting their attendance in person or in writing, do so in a manner that allows them enough time to process their thoughts, but not *so* much time that they dwell on the upcoming meeting.

Issuing personal invitations

Your employees may not yet see a mediated conversation as a helpful and constructive thing, and that usually means resistance. If you choose to approach them in person, do so in a private and confidential way. Find a time when each employee is alone and has a few moments to chat with you. They'll both likely have a number of questions, so allow some time for them to process the request and come back to you if they feel the need.

The benefits to a face-to-face meeting request include the following:

- ✔ **Your employees have the opportunity to hear from you firsthand what your intentions are for the dialogue.** They'll likely initially see this conversation as a disciplinary action, rather than as an opportunity to solve problems. You can do a lot to reinforce a positive, creative approach to the conversation ahead of time, simply by talking about the meeting as just such an opportunity.

- ✔ **Your employees have a chance to process with you how they're thinking and feeling in real time.** Processing those thoughts and feelings now is better than brooding and worrying over the course of a few days while they prepare for the meeting.

If you offer a verbal invite to your meeting, you may begin to hear more than you're ready for right away. Knowing that a mediated conversation is imminent, employees may try to deflect or defer the meeting. They may even try to convince you that the other one is clearly the problem. If that happens, just reiterate your desire to talk about anything they'd like to share during the meeting and tell them that, for now, you're just letting them know the particulars and your expectations for the meeting.

A personal invitation is *not* the best bet if you're not comfortable relaying all the details about the meeting and people's roles within it. In that case, use the written option (see the next section).

Sending written invitations

Putting the meeting request in writing provides your employees time to consider their reactions and thoughts before engaging anyone in discussion.

You know your workplace, and you know what's appropriate and not appropriate when it comes to written meeting requests. If possible, make this invitation informal rather than formal. An email or personal note is better than written instructions on company letterhead using very businesslike language. The best-written invitations are simple, personal and confidential.

Provide both employees with an opportunity to talk to you if they have any questions or concerns. You don't want them going into your meeting with false impressions or preconceived ideas about your intentions and goals.

A written invitation has some limitations. Specifically, the employees may be concerned about

- The formality of such a meeting
- Who else knows about the conflict or the meetings
- Whether your email or letter will be part of their permanent files
- Whether their jobs are at stake

Anticipate concerns and include those items in the text of your invitation. Put their minds at ease with language that's clear, concise and inviting.

Here's an example of a written invitation that includes concepts I go over throughout this chapter. Your memo should look something like this:

> Dear Barbara and Pat,
>
> Thank you for spending a few minutes to talk with me the other day about the conflict you're experiencing. I know this hasn't been an easy time for you, so I've arranged for the three of us to meet on Tuesday at 9.30 am in the level 1 conference room. My intention in calling this meeting is to mediate a conversation in which you'll both be able to share ideas on how we might resolve the issues. Your attendance is mandatory, but I'd like you both to voluntarily prepare a number of ideas for possible solutions.
>
> During the meeting, I'll act as a neutral facilitator. That means I won't be taking sides, and nor will I be advocating for one idea over another. If at any point you feel it's necessary for me to act in a managerial capacity to determine how a particular idea might play out, I'll

certainly be able to do that. Otherwise, consider this *your* meeting with *your* agenda.

Our department head has asked that I report the result of the meeting to her, and I've agreed. I will not, however, be sharing anything other than whether an agreement is reached and what follow-up is needed. I would like you both to keep the meeting to yourselves, and we can decide who else needs to know about the outcome at the end of our discussion.

I expect that you both will come prepared to discuss all the pertinent topics and that you'll be open and willing to hear what each other has to say. Between now and the meeting, consider your specific issues, possible solutions to the problems and how you'll respectfully communicate these things to each other.

Clear your calendar for the better part of the day. I'll have lunch brought in so we won't have any distractions. This meeting is a priority for me, so I'll make sure I'm not interrupted. Please do the same.

I'm confident you each have what it takes to work this out. If you both give this your best effort and you're not able to resolve the problem, I can offer additional resources. If I can clear up any questions you have about the meeting details, please let me know. Otherwise, anything you'd like to share about the situation should be saved for the meeting.

Explaining your role

In your (verbal or written) communication about your meeting, discuss and clarify your dual roles in the meeting. You'll need to act both as a manager and a mediator, but for very different reasons and at very different times.

At times, you may need to clarify policies and procedures that are specific to your workplace. The majority of the time, however, you'll want to be acting in a different role. Instead of 'the boss', you want them to see you as both of the following:

- ✔ **Facilitator:** Essentially, you'll be facilitating the conversation. This means that you won't be taking anyone's side or speaking on behalf of either party.

- ✔ **Guide:** This means that the responsibility for making all the decisions comes down to your employees.

If your employees can see you as a facilitator and a guide rather than as an enforcer of policies or a disciplinarian, they'll be more likely to speak openly and thoughtfully, and think creatively about possible solutions.

Helping employees get into the right frame of mind

When you invite the parties to the meeting, you can do a couple of things to prepare them and to help them create some opportunities that will make this conversation go well.

Consider the following:

- ✔ **Ask them to come fully prepared to discuss all the topics that are pertinent to their conflict.** Encourage them to be open and willing to discuss any possible items that may come up, to think creatively and come to the meeting with a number of ideas for resolving the issues.

- ✔ **Remind them to be aware of their language — which includes tone of voice and body language.** The best conversations are ones in which your employees, though they may disagree with each other, speak respectfully and without interruption.

This part of your process really only serves as a means to get the parties in the right frame of mind prior to the meeting. You'll be repeating these instructions again in a much more formalised fashion when the meeting begins.

Assuring confidentiality

Start by addressing the extent to which you'll be acting in a confidential manner. Specifically, clarify with your employees exactly what you *will* and *won't* share with others. If you'll be reporting to your manager the results of the discussion, be clear and upfront about it.

Additionally, you must address the confidentiality expectations you have of the employees. Because others are likely interested in this conversation, you need to tell the parties involved how they should speak about the upcoming meeting with the rest of the staff (if they talk about it at all). Encourage them to limit any conversation with others regarding your meeting or the person they're in conflict with.

When you're in the meeting (see Chapter 7 for more about the actual meeting), you can create some specific and mutually agreed-upon language surrounding the confidentiality of the conversation. For now, however, you're just trying to do some damage control and limit the problems that can arise when other employees throw in their two cents.

Defining meeting parameters

Having a clear understanding of the degree to which this process is voluntary or mandatory is important. If possible (and doing so works in with any formalised dispute resolution procedure your organisation may have), I encourage you to describe this meeting as mandatory with voluntary elements.

Let employees know that you're expecting them to attend, participate fully and give it their best efforts, but that they are *not* required to reach a solution at any cost during the session. Also, though the meeting may be mandatory, any offers they make or solutions they arrive at are entirely voluntary. Discuss this point in the meeting request to alleviate any fears that they'll be stuck in a room for hours only to finally give in just so they can leave. Let them know that other options are available if they come to a standstill.

Giving pre-work/homework instructions

Your invitation to the meeting should include some specific tasks the parties can work on in the days leading up to the conversation. Consider the following topics as possible pre-work:

- ✔ **Specific issues:** Encourage employees to spend some time identifying specific behaviours and issues that upset them, so they can put language to their conflict.

- ✔ **Language:** Encourage employees to be thoughtful of the *way* in which they discuss their concerns, and to find language that expresses their concerns without making the other person defensive or resistant.

- ✔ **Possible solutions:** You want your employees to be open to ideas and proposals that are generated through brainstorming within the meeting, but it never hurts to have them prepare some ideas in advance. Ask them to think about what would make them *most* satisfied *and* what they'd be willing to live with.

✔ **Their own responsibility:** Help employees see that their own responsibility — what they're willing to do —is not so much a concession, but a strategy. Can they think of anything they may be able to do to bring the conflict to an agreeable close?

Setting Up the Meeting

Before your employees are ready to sit down with you and get the conversation started, you have some work to do. By preparing the space for your meeting, you maximise your potential for a successful conversation.

Choosing a neutral location

You must maintain the appearance and substance of neutrality at all times throughout your conversation. Any suggestion — whether real or imagined — that you've compromised neutrality will derail your process. (For more information about neutrality, see Chapter 7.)

Here are a few things you can do to create a sense of safety and neutrality:

✔ **Consider the location of the room itself.** Try not to schedule your meeting in any location that could be described as either employee's 'turf'. Work to balance the power early to avoid having to address a power struggle during the meeting.

You may think that your office is the ideal spot but, the truth is, your office only reinforces the idea that this meeting is a disciplinary action — which is a message to avoid.

✔ **Choose a meeting room that's as private as possible.** Meeting someplace where other employees are wandering in and out or lurking (and listening) won't create the kind of environment you want. Avoid meeting rooms in a high-traffic area and/or with lots of windows — instead, find a place where the curious eyes of others won't affect your discussion.

Private should also mean minimal distractions. A room with a telephone constantly ringing or computer beeps announcing the arrival of new email serves only to distract from the conversation. Listening well is hard when you have distractions competing for your attention.

Allowing enough time

Successful mediated conversations take some time. If you're following the process in this book and following each step to its fullest potential, your conversation may take upwards of three to four hours (including the occasional ten- to fifteen-minute breaks you'll take for personal needs).

Make sure that the parties allow for such a time commitment when you schedule the meeting. You want them to treat this meeting as a priority, not an afterthought. It's reasonable to assume that the demands of the workplace may intervene in the conversation, but setting clear expectations about the importance of the meeting should create the space for the parties to devote enough time to reach solid agreements.

Facilitating a comfortable environment

These kinds of conversations can be difficult and uncomfortable for employees. You can help create a more positive response to the conversation, however, by improving the comfort of your surroundings.

Holding the meeting on neutral ground is important, but location is only part of that equation. Both of your employees must have equal access to all the amenities that you provide. Yes, it sounds silly to discuss these finer details, but trust me, they matter. I had a mediation go south right from the start because one party's pen didn't work and the other person couldn't stop laughing!

Consider the quantity and quality of everything in the meeting. For example, if you provide three pieces of paper to one employee, make sure the other employee also has three pieces of paper. If you provide a black pen with a cap to one, make sure that the other person has the same. Any indication of partiality can disrupt your process.

Make the process go more smoothly by setting up your room in a fairly bare-bones way. The fewer distractions the better. That said, consider including a few of the following items to help the parties make the most of their time:

- **Blank paper:** To jot down any notes or thoughts they have during the process, or for documenting important decisions that come from your discussion. This is also a great way to remind your employees not to interrupt each other when they're speaking. By drawing attention to the paper, you can subtly remind them to wait their turn.

- **Pens/pencils:** If you're going to have paper, make sure to provide something they can write with. Oh, and make sure that both pens work or that both pencils are equally sharp!

- **Comfortable chairs:** The meeting is going to last approximately three to four hours, so provide comfortable chairs. Lengthy and difficult conversations can be made even *more* lengthy and difficult if you're constantly readjusting, trying to find a comfortable position.

- **Water and snacks:** Your employees may appreciate some simple amenities like water when their voices get tired from talking, or something to munch on to help keep their blood sugar stable. Providing water and snacks also prevents the need for too many breaks.

    Some snacks are better than others. Nervous employees who gobble down handful after handful of lollies may have a quick burst of energy followed about an hour later by a pretty nasty sugar crash. I provide protein bars or muesli bars and a small bowl of confectionary.

- **Tissues:** Don't be surprised if you see tears from either of your employees. It may not happen, but if it does, you need to be prepared. And acknowledging upfront that your employees might cry can put them more at ease — and so reduce the likelihood of tears.

- **A way to keep time:** You may keep a clock in the room with you for the purposes of monitoring the length and timing of your meeting. Because you'll be the facilitator of the process, your employees having access to a clock is less important. If you do provide one, however, just make sure each employee has equal access to it.

Preparing Yourself

With all the work you've done to prepare your employees, you also need to take a few minutes to focus on yourself. Getting caught up in the conflict is pretty easy to do. Don't allow yourself to get overinvested in the outcome, though. In fact, the less emotionally invested you are, the better.

This is your employees' conflict. They own the problems, so they own the solutions! If you allow yourself to become attached to the conflict and you become invested enough to make suggestions or offer solutions, you've effectively become responsible for those outcomes and whether they succeed or fail. Your employees will be more likely to buy in and follow through on an agreement when they themselves propose and refine it.

Before your meeting begins, take about 30 minutes to prepare yourself for what's to come. Strong conflict creates strong emotions, not only on the part of the participants but also for any observer. Expect to hear language that's affected by emotions, and prepare yourself accordingly.

Prepare yourself in these three ways while waiting for your meeting to begin:

- ✔ **Mentally:** Be ready to listen for facts, figures and timelines so you can keep it all straight in your own mind. Be sure to clear whatever time is necessary for your meeting. If you can, take care of any issues that may be hanging over you. You won't be giving your best to your employees if you're thinking about your own project that's due at the end of the week!

- ✔ **Emotionally:** This is the self-preparation that comes with expecting to hear difficult language and raised voices. Remind yourself who the conflict really belongs to (your employees!) and who is responsible for solving the problem (them!). This approach will help centre you before the meeting.

- ✔ **Personally:** Whatever helps you clear your mind and focus on the present will help you make the most of your time in the coming meeting. Anyone who does mediation for a living knows that high emotions and negative energy can exhaust even the most prepared facilitator, so some people I know meditate, some read over a favourite passage and others listen to music. I prefer complete silence before I bring parties in.

Chapter 7

Starting a Mediation Meeting and Creating a Working Agenda

· ·

In This Chapter

▶ Kicking off a mediation meeting

▶ Reminding employees about roles and responsibilities

▶ Listening to employees' perspectives

▶ Summarising, reflecting and reframing

▶ Preparing a road map for discussion

· ·

*I*n this chapter, I give you skills and techniques to direct
the conversation in a meaningful way as well as step-by-step
instructions on how to demonstrate your neutrality by reflecting
emotions and issues back to the parties. I also share tips on
ordering and structuring a productive agenda.

Facilitating Effectively

Mediating a discussion is about reading the situation in a way
that puts you in the facilitator's seat but allows you enough
involvement in the discussion to move the conversation
forward. It's not refereeing; it's guiding. And it's guiding without
the parties feeling manipulated. Stay on top of the conversation
without getting too involved in it.

Establishing rapport and making employees comfortable

Your employees need to see you as a neutral and impartial facilitator of their dialogue, even if you're required to wear the Manager Hat when you leave the room.

The words you choose and the tone you take set the stage for either a productive conversation or a gripe session to ensue. Draw on the following tips to establish rapport and make everyone feel comfortable:

- ✔ **Use open language.** Use words that encourage positive interactions, like share, create, explore, encourage, clarify and guide. Avoid words that detract or shut down interactions, like must, require, expect, demand and impose.

- ✔ **Be brief.** Your opening comments should be lengthy enough to describe the process and expectations but not so long that you lose their interest.

- ✔ **Project confidence.** If you appear nervous or uncomfortable, you may send a signal to your employees that they, too, should be nervous or uncomfortable.

Showing your neutrality

Present yourself as neutrally as possible. If the time arises when you have to step back into the management role and make a decision, the decision will be better received if the employees feel you were impartial during the rest of the conversation.

Here are some easy ways to show and keep an impartial role in the process:

- ✔ **Position yourself in the middle.** Your chair should be in a position that maintains an easy balance between the parties.

- ✔ **Strive for balanced eye contact.** Spend most of your time connecting with the person who's speaking, but be sure to check in periodically with the other person.

- ✔ **Watch your reactions.** A raised eyebrow, a rolled eye or a dropped jaw at the wrong moment can send a pretty clear message that you've made up your mind and have lost your objectivity.

✔ **Balance your feedback.** Keep your feedback roughly in balance in terms of timing, tone and content. For tips on giving feedback, see 'Summarising and Reflecting Back What You Hear', later in this chapter).

✔ **Facilitate dialogue.** Your job is to give participants the space to create their own conversation, to acknowledge and validate their perspectives, and to facilitate them solving their own problem.

Actively listening

While each party tells you what's been going on for them, demonstrate that you hear and understand what the speaker is sharing by doing the following:

✔ Display open body language by assuming a comfortable posture with your arms at your sides or resting on the table.

✔ Try to lean forward just enough to demonstrate your interest but not so much that you're sitting in the speaker's lap.

✔ Be aware of environmental impacts on your body language. If you've folded your arms because the temperature of the room is chilly, a participant could read that as a judgemental posture.

✔ Take simple notes (not a word-for-word transcript) on what each speaker is saying, but also listen carefully for any values and emotions you hear. Make note of important dates, numbers or other facts, and take special care to note any potential common ground that the two parties share.

It's difficult for a listening co-worker not to interrupt, so make sure you're doing enough to stay connected in some way with her. Simple movements like a glance in her direction or sliding your hand toward her side of the table can be enough to say that you haven't forgotten that she's there and that in a moment you'll be sure to provide her an opportunity to speak about her perspective.

Saving your questions for later

You may be tempted to ask a number of questions while your parties are sharing their thoughts. Resist that urge! This meeting isn't an inquisition, so wait until later to test assumptions or address misinformation. Chapter 8 explains more on how to do that.

This part of the meeting isn't about the facts; it's about the experience. You want your participants to feel open to share information. Your only job here is to make sure that you're hearing and understanding what's said.

Reviewing the Ground Rules for the Discussion

Set the right tone for the meeting from the start. Your participants need to be clear in your expectations of them and as comfortable as is reasonably possible. Bring them in together, and begin by inviting both of them to take a moment to relax as you outline some of the housekeeping items that will make the meeting run smoother. Set up the parameters by using clear language in an organised and professional manner. With that said, don't freak everybody out by being so scripted that it sounds like they're on trial. Set boundaries, but let the employees know you're willing to be flexible.

If this is the first time the two have been able to talk, be aware that a lot of new information will be exchanged, and it's up to you to make sure they're really hearing what the other has to say. On the other hand, if they've tried talking to one another before, they've probably shared most of the details but can't agree on a solution. If the latter is the case, let them know you'll focus on helping them brainstorm solutions that work for both sides.

Also let them know that you'll spend most of the time together understanding from each person what keeps them in conflict and then working to find what each needs in order to limit further problems. For now they've probably prepared some pretty tough language about the other person (or even regarding their thoughts about this meeting) that may threaten to derail your process. But don't panic! Go over rules of common courtesy, and point out that you won't tolerate name-calling or disrespectful language.

Emphasise collaboration by stressing to your employees that this conversation is their opportunity to come together and work on a solution that's satisfactory to both of them. Include language that emphasises the responsibility that each shares in brainstorming and implementing solutions.

In this section, I walk you through a sound way to describe what's about to happen, what you will and won't be doing for each of your participants, and what you expect from everyone at the table.

Explaining roles and responsibilities

Explain that, as mediator, you aren't acting as a decision-maker, an advocate or even a counsellor. You're here to help them explore their issues and concerns, assist them in brainstorming options, and aid them in creating their own mutually agreeable outcomes and solutions.

This is not your conflict! If you become invested in the outcome, take sides, or offer solutions and ideas, you risk alienating one (or both!) employees. Additionally, if your ideas or suggestions don't meet their needs, in their eyes you may effectively become responsible for the failure of the process.

After you state your role, clearly stress the importance of the participants' roles and responsibilities. Specifically, outline the kind of behaviour you'd like to see from them during the course of the conversation. Discuss these key points:

- ✔ **Willingness to listen:** Asking employees to communicate respectfully means allowing time to finish sentences and thoughts without interrupting, and not monopolising the floor when speaking.

- ✔ **Willingness to share:** Encourage them to speak from their own perspectives. Remind them that hearing what each person has to say is important and that this meeting is a safe setting in which to do so.

- ✔ **Courteous treatment:** Ask your employees to remember that courteous treatment of one another is a simple way to make your meeting go smoother.

- ✔ **Openness to new ideas:** Although each employee has likely come to this meeting with only one way of addressing the conflict, encourage them to remember that problems can be solved in multiple ways.

Directing the flow of information

Encourage your participants to start out by speaking directly to you. They'll have an opportunity to speak to one another later but, for now, you want all their energy and attention focused on you. They likely have prepared scripts running in their heads, which include a laundry list of things that the other person has done, and they may use language that isn't terribly helpful. Rather than have them lob this language at one another, ask them to give it to *you*.

Stressing uninterrupted time

Uninterrupted time means that while one person is speaking, the other is listening. Encourage your employees to honour this approach, rather than calling them out on interruptions. If you blurt out, 'Don't interrupt!', you dismiss the fact that the topic is uncomfortable for the interrupter. You may have to be stern later if they continue to talk over one another, but the best first step is to ask them to jot down their thoughts for when it's their turn to speak.

Giving the Participants a Chance to Present Their Perspectives

At the start of the meeting, your employees are likely concentrating on what they're going to say, what they're going to keep to themselves, and how they're really going to let the other person have it when it's their turn to talk. From the moment the first person opens his mouth, your job is to move them from blaming to eventually creating solutions. Do this by listening to both parties, pulling out pertinent information, acknowledging emotions and neutralising statements.

Deciding who speaks first

Ask the parties which of them would like to speak first, and allow them to make that choice on their own. Be patient and allow them some time and space to work it out. If they still struggle, comment on the fact that going first has no benefit (and neither does second, for that matter) and ask for a volunteer.

Watch for power moves. An employee may bully her way into speaking first, or she could gallantly let her co-worker go first because she feels certain she'll be able to rip his perspective to shreds. A quick check with the other person ('Is that okay with you?') lets him know it really is a joint decision.

Listening to the second participant

After the first employee has had a chance to express his thoughts, take the time to summarise what you heard (see the next section 'Summarising and Reflecting Back What You Hear' for details). Then turn your attention to the second party. Start by thanking the first party for his statement and the other party for waiting and being patient (even if she really hasn't shown a lot of patience!). Reaffirm that this is the second party's chance to share her thoughts, and then put some additional parameters around your expectations.

Tell the second party that although she may be tempted to respond to what the first speaker has just said, you want her to speak as if she's sharing first. This mindset gives her an opportunity to present her story in a fuller way.

After the second employee has shared her point of view and you've reflected back to her, turn your attention back to the first party and say, 'Would you like to add anything that hasn't already been discussed or respond to a particular point?' It's my experience that any more than one response during opening statements just makes for a prolonged back-and-forth that looks more like a tennis match than a productive conversation.

You may find that your parties attempt to begin the negotiation process here by turning to one another and bypassing you as a facilitator. You need to prevent this from happening because it can seriously derail the meeting, but bear in mind that this action is actually good news! It means that your parties are active and engaged and ready to get to work, so use their desire to talk to each other to your advantage. To guide the conversation back on track, say something like, 'I can see that the two of you are anxious to get started. Let's complete this part of the process and then we'll move forward.'

Summarising and Reflecting Back What You Hear

After the first party shares his perspective, briefly summarise what you've heard before moving to the other person. Likewise, after you listen to the second person, summarise before giving the first person a chance to speak again. Summarising not only allows the speaker to know that you've heard and understood what he had to say but also gives the other employee the opportunity to hear the concerns from a new source (you) and with new ears.

In the following sections, I show you how to reflect emotions, reframe statements and neutralise perspectives. Each of these skills on its own makes up only a small portion of the kind of feedback to provide participants at the end of their statements. The truth is, you need to combine all the elements together into one succinct, summarised package. You can use each of these skills independently, but bringing them all together works best.

Reflecting, reframing and neutralising take some practice. Focus on the core message in what you're hearing. In the meeting, take some time and be reflective about how you'd like to say what you're thinking. Try not to worry so much about getting it *exactly* right. If you're pretty close, you'll see subtle clues and hints that your summaries resonate. If you notice quizzical looks, furrowed brows or a shaking head, feel free to ask for an opportunity to try it again.

Be careful not to use the same language over and over again. You may become very comfortable framing responses in a certain way, but it can be distracting for the listener. For instance, you've probably heard someone start a reflecting statement with, 'It sounds like you're feeling . . .' In and of itself that's good language, but you start to sound artificial if you use the same phrase all the time.

Find different ways to frame your response, such as:

'It sounds like . . .'

'I hear [blank] is important to you.'

'You feel strongly about [blank].'

'When you said [blank], I understood . . .'

'So for you it's important to . . .'

Reflecting emotions

Conflicts create strong feelings. Recognising emotions and speaking to them in others is important, so as the mediator of the conversation you need to spend some time understanding how to reflect another person's feelings.

Reflecting is about putting a voice to the emotions that you see or hear, and it creates an openness and curiosity about the emotions you may not observe.

To reflect effectively, start by identifying what you think the speaker's emotion may be. For example, imagine that you're mediating a conflict between Carol and Peter. In the midst of her opening statement, Carol says, 'Peter never finishes any of the projects he starts, but he's always there to get the accolades when we finish.'

What are Carol's emotions? How is she feeling? She certainly sounds pretty frustrated, annoyed and maybe even a little disappointed. When you relay your understanding of her emotions back in a way that allows her to know she's been heard, you're halfway to understanding why this conflict has had such an impact on her.

Here are some examples of effective reflecting:

> Statement: 'I can't believe she botched another presentation!'
>
> Reflected: 'You're concerned that the presentations haven't gone well.'
>
> Statement: 'She places way too much demand on us. We can't do it all!'
>
> Reflected: 'It's been difficult to accomplish all the assigned tasks.'
>
> Statement: 'Our project was an utter failure. He really screwed it up.'
>
> Reflected: 'You're disappointed at the way the project turned out.'

Notice that in the examples, nothing is intentionally said about what was supposedly wrong about the other person. The idea is simply to speak to what the speaker is feeling. It may be true that she's frustrated because of the other person, but the point of effective reflecting is to highlight the emotion itself.

You may have also noticed that in the reflection, the emotion is toned down just slightly from what the speaker describes. That's intentional, too. Your goal is to soften the language used to help reduce the emotion so the participants can create the kind of conversation that moves them forward. For example, if you hear 'angry' and reflect instead 'frustration', you're purposefully acknowledging emotion while calming the situation. Similarly, you may hear 'crushed' and reflect instead 'disappointed'. Reflecting just below where you think the emotion may be goes a long way in softening the participant who's experiencing the emotion.

Conversely, if you hear an emotion and reflect it more strongly, you run the risk of taking the speaker beyond that emotion. For instance, if you hear 'anger' and reflect instead 'rage', you may find the speaker using much stronger language and, in fact, becoming angrier than she was before!

Reframing statements

Parties involved in mediations have a tendency to talk about the things they don't like or disapprove of in each other rather than what's personally important to them. Reframing is a way to capture what's important to the speaker while leaving out what's supposedly wrong with the other person.

Reframing is also a way of highlighting and drawing out interests or values, which is a tremendous asset to you as a facilitator. (Check out Chapter 2 for a definition and explanation of values.) Highlighting the values shifts the conversation away from negative descriptions and toward describing what's important to each party; this allows your participants to talk about the same thing without requiring them to see it the same way.

Here are some examples of statements and their reframed summaries:

> Statement: 'He never shares any information. I don't understand why he can't just provide me with the numbers.'
>
> Reframed: 'It's important for you to work cooperatively.'

Statement: 'She's so dismissive of everyone's proposals. She always says "no" to everything and insults us when we come up with ideas.'

Reframed: 'You'd like to have a respectful talk about proposals.'

Statement: 'She has to create a timeline for everything! I have to juggle multiple projects, and I don't need her trying to make my work process fit into her little plan.'

Reframed: 'You'd prefer the ability to work to your own schedule and at your own pace. Autonomy is important to you.'

By reframing language to include the values you hear, you create the opportunity to discuss what each value means to the parties. Then they can begin to think about how they may be able to ask for the important things they've described rather than only asking for resolution to a surface issue. For example, asking someone to respect a need for autonomy is a much different request than asking her to quit checking the reports.

Neutralising the perspectives

When summarising statements and providing feedback, neutralise difficult language to take the sting out of words without taking away from the message. You can capture the spirit of a message without minimising or downplaying the meaning.

Here are some examples of statements and their neutralised summaries:

Statement: 'That meeting was a total catastrophe.'

Neutralised: 'The meeting didn't go as you had hoped.'

Statement: 'We got into a shouting match in front of the staff.'

Neutralised: 'There was a loud conversation that others observed.'

Statement: 'The project has hit a total dead end. It's done for.'

Neutralised: 'The project is facing some difficulties.'

Creating an Agenda

You may be wondering why I'm asking you to create an agenda midway through your meeting process. What gives? Well, an *agenda* in mediation is *not* a pre-generated list of topics that you use to guide the discussion. Nor is it a schedule of events and activities for your dialogue. Instead, it's a list of topics the employees want to talk about that they collaboratively create after hearing each other's perspective. By generating the list together, they're much more likely to see each topic as belonging to both of them rather than feeling that you're forcing topics on them.

The agenda creation is about clarifying and naming issues and creating a road map for the discussion that's to come. This is your opportunity to help put some structure to the conversation.

Start by standing up and moving to a whiteboard or easel. Tell the parties it's time to build a meeting agenda that will cover the topics and issues that are important to them. They talk; you write. (Manage what gets written down so you can ensure that inflammatory or hurtful language stays off the list.)

In the following sections, I show you how to take what might seem like a random stream of consciousness from the parties and turn it into an organised list. The agenda is your silent co-mediator and helps you keep the parties on track and further define issues, and it acts as a visual reminder of their progress.

Transitioning from the past to the future

Use the agenda to make an important point: It's time to move from the past to the future. Set the stage for the conversation to come by saying, 'Thank you for sharing your perspectives. As we begin to build an agenda, keep in mind that you'll discuss each of these items thoroughly, but you'll do so with a focus on the future rather than rehashing the past.' Your statement should focus the employees to move them away from where the problems have been and head toward where the solutions are.

Demonstrating accessibility and ownership

As you begin to create the agenda, make sure the list is visible to both employees, meaning that one won't be able to look directly at it while the other has to crane his neck to see it. In effect, your employees should be facing almost the same direction, working side by side. Also, make sure both participants know that they can add to the list at any time and that it's flexible. It should be seen as a living document rather than etched in stone.

Whatever you do, don't let go of the marker! Take responsibility for creating and editing the list so one of your employees doesn't hijack the process by erasing all your hard work or adding language that derails the conversation.

Let the parties know that they don't need to agree on the topics listed on the agenda. In other words, if one wants to have a conversation about a topic, it goes on the list as a potential topic for discussion. This point is important, because it creates ownership in the topics an employee suggests and in her co-worker's suggestions as well.

Separating their topics

Chances are the parties will see all the difficulties they're having as one big mess and lump everything into the same category on the agenda list.

Unravel complicated agenda suggestions by asking questions. Don't rush to write something down. Instead, take a few minutes to gently challenge your employees to give you more. For example, ask what someone means when he says that he wants to talk about 'the problem'. How would he break that down into a small handful of specific topics?

Labelling and defining issues

Your employees need to see the agenda list as belonging to both of them rather than see each topic as either 'mine' or 'not mine'. So when possible, point out commonalities and reiterate that this is a collaborative agenda.

Make sure all the topics you list are neutral and presented objectively. Creating neutral topics is an important part of generating buy-in to the process. But if you're relying on the parties to create the topics, how can you expect them to keep the list civil? The truth is, you may not be able to. What you can do, though, is reframe their language to make it more palatable.

Say one of your participants says that she wants to talk about the fact that the staff meetings run way too long and end up in shouting matches. She wants to cut the meetings in half and has a pretty good plan to make it work. But the other participant quickly responds that, in fact, the meetings are a necessary way of exchanging ideas and information, and extending the time would help make sure everyone is on the same page about projects.

If you list the topic as 'Cut staff meetings in half', you've essentially recorded a position (or solution) that's only one person's way of resolving the issue. And if you list 'Extend staff meetings', you've done the same thing in reverse. So what's really the topic here? The staff meeting is what's important, so list that. How the participants feel and what they think about the meeting remains intact, and neither of them is alienated by the topic as it appears on the agenda.

Make sure the agenda includes all the issues. You don't want to finish the meeting only to realise a key issue has gone unnoticed and unaddressed. Ask both parties after the list is made if they need to discuss anything else in order to find a resolution, and remind them that items can be added or erased later.

Considering common agenda topics

Although it's true that every facilitated conversation is different depending on the participants and their concerns, a few common themes tend to surface when dealing with work issues. Having some sample language at the ready helps you frame topics in an objective, constructive manner. I use the following agenda topics quite often:

> ✔ **Roles and responsibilities:** This topic can describe a number of situations in which employees see their job responsibilities differently. Put this on the board if you need to discuss disagreements about job descriptions and areas of influence.

✔ **Respect:** Another common theme in workplace scenarios is the hard-to-define yet all-important concept of what respect means to employees. Although each party is likely to describe it differently, they get an opportunity to speak about how they wish to be respected and what it means to show respect to others.

✔ **Communication:** This agenda topic is a simple way to discuss differences in how employees speak to one another. Many workplace conflicts boil down to either a lack of communication or different approaches to communication.

✔ **Confidentiality:** Confidentiality is huge in mediation, so even if your employees don't bring it up, you should. This is a great topic that covers other employees' interest or curiosity in what's happening in the meeting or when to share details about the conflict.

Using the agenda for negotiations

The agenda helps you structure brainstorming, aids in problem-solving, and creates an organised way to kick off negotiations (check out Chapter 8 for a discussion of the negotiating process). Breaking the conflict into smaller pieces helps your employees feel the situation is a little more manageable.

The agenda is a tool you'll use throughout the negotiation and agreement phases, and it will serve you best in these areas if you

✔ Have the parties choose one item at a time to discuss.

✔ Be thorough with each item and do your best to work through one topic completely before moving on to another.

✔ Move on to another point if the two participants get stuck on something. You can always come back to the topic later.

✔ Talk about each and every concern on the list.

Chapter 8

Negotiating Possible Solutions to a Conflict

. . . .

In This Chapter

▶ Getting employees to open up

▶ Homing in on values

▶ Brainstorming to generate ideas

▶ Posing the right questions

▶ Overcoming common conflict obstacles

▶ Meeting with each participant confidentially

. . . .

*N*egotiating any sort of resolution to conflict is tricky. You need to continue to listen and adapt to whatever your employees need to assess their unique situation while they shift into the negotiation phase of the meeting.

In this chapter, I give you the information you need to move your employees beyond a list of discussion topics onto collaboratively addressing the conflict and brainstorming possible solutions. You also find tools to work through resistance so you can reposition your employees from a state of blaming one another to a problem-solving mindset, creatively enabling them to tackle future difficulties using a new skill set.

Encouraging Communication

At this stage of the meeting, you need to be flexible and adapt to wherever your employees take you while keeping in mind some overarching guidelines that focus and organise the conversation. Keep the parties talking, but guide them to stay positive, think creatively and move beyond their immediate problems. Talking in circles never gets anyone anywhere. This section helps you steer the conversation in the right direction.

Transitioning from past to future

When asked earlier to share their points of view, your employees probably spent a lot of time talking about the past (refer to Chapter 7). Now it's time for them to begin moving forward. Make a statement about moving out of the past and into the present so you can set the stage for dialogue about solutions rather than problems.

To get employees to talk about the future, use the agenda they created as a visual tool (refer to Chapter 7) by standing next to it or pointing to it. Then say something like, 'Looking at the list you've created, I'd like the two of you to choose a topic together and decide where you'd like to begin your conversation. Stay focused on what you'd like to see, and try not to rehash what's already taken place.'

Motivating and encouraging your employees

Conversations about conflicts are hard work. Creating a dialogue in the midst of problems takes courage and energy, so validate and praise your employees for their efforts and find ways to acknowledge the good work they accomplish. In other words, encourage the behaviour you *want to see* more than discourage the behaviour you *don't want to see*.

Look for areas of common ground between your employees — after all, both are likely frustrated with the situation, and anxious to get some solutions on the table. You could note that each has a stake and a responsibility in creating a stable and comfortable workplace. And anytime that you detect values they have in common — like respect or autonomy — point them out. Allow them to talk about how they define those values differently and what actions need to be taken for those values to be fulfilled.

Emphasise that this discussion is an opportunity to create what they want their ongoing relationship to look like. Encourage them to see the conversation as a turning point in their interaction with each other rather than as a trial for you to judge who makes the better case.

Listening and interjecting

The negotiation process is about your employees working together to create their own answer to the conflict. Do more listening than speaking and, when you do interject, use the strategies I outline in the following sections.

Ask questions

The majority of the speaking you do should come in the form of good questions (see the section 'Asking Great Questions', later in this chapter, for more information). Focus on encouraging your employees to negotiate together rather than on drawing their attention to you.

Clarify and summarise

Listen for any language that threatens to derail the process, such as blaming, antagonising, pushing hot buttons or name-calling. Be aware, however, that because of the emotional state your employees are in, they may be more apt to misinterpret or misunderstand what the other person says. If you hear your employees struggling with language, summarise what you've heard with more neutral language and help them clarify their intent.

If the words your employees use are downright hostile, intervene by reflecting their emotions, reframing their language to focus on their interests, and neutralising any provocative language you hear. Remind the speaker that he made a commitment to follow the ground rules for this meeting, and warn him that he needs to manage the way he speaks about his emotions.

Capture proposals

When you hear proposed solutions from either party (see the 'Fostering Brainstorming' section, later in this chapter), summarise the important points and frame them in language that's easy for the other party to digest. Ask the other party what she likes or doesn't like about the proposal, whether she accepts it as is, or if she'd like to make a counter proposal.

Make note of any possible proposals you hear that the employees may not be quite ready to offer. Doing so gives you a reference point down the road, when they begin to make a little more progress.

Focusing on Values Rather Than Issues

During the course of the meeting, you're likely to hear a lot from both people that describes how the conflict should be resolved. The language will likely come in the form of a position they've taken, also known as their *issues*.

You need to hear and understand the issues, because they give you a sense of the nature of the conflict. However, understanding why those issues are of importance to your employees is more crucial. As such, you need to focus more on discovering their values — the things that drive them to act the way they do and make the decisions they choose. (Refer to Chapter 2 for an extensive list and information about how values surface in the workplace.)

The following sections help you drill beneath the surface of your employees' issues and draw out the values that are at the heart of their conflict.

Discovering what's really important

Employees often come to a mediation meeting with a win–lose approach in mind, arguing about the merits of each other's position. By focusing the conversation on values, you can help them find common interests — or at least those that aren't in conflict — and develop a collaborative approach to negotiating. This moves them away from what they *don't like* and nudges them toward what they *would like*.

Understanding and validating your employees' values helps you identify and articulate appropriate responses to emotional outbursts. Acknowledging these values is the best intervention strategy in many conflict resolutions.

Reading between the lines to find values

Uncovering values takes a little work. The key is to listen for what lies beneath the statements your employees make. Tune your ear to strip away the things you hear them saying, and listen instead for what drives their positions. For example, if someone gets upset when a colleague is late for meetings, what's likely important to them is that schedules are respected. Timeliness is likely something they very much value.

Responding to a person about what he values rather than adding to the criticism of what the other person has done wrong allows the second party to explain her view of the situation without becoming defensive. When you reframe and reflect a person's statement, you also model good communication for both people. To get more familiar with effective reframing and reflecting, check out Chapter 7.

Fostering Brainstorming

Good brainstorming motivates your employees to think creatively about problem-solving, lets them know that this is their process and reminds them that there's no *one right way* to solve difficulties. The following sections give you some brainstorming guidelines and help you evaluate the results of your efforts.

Defining brainstorming ground rules

Encourage your employees to view brainstorming as an opportunity to create any kind of solutions they can imagine. Give them the freedom to suggest anything and you'll find that their ideas and proposals are as creative as they are effective.

The best brainstorming occurs without limits to creativity but focuses on one area at a time. Suggest a few ground rules, such as:

- ✔ **Use the agenda:** Ask participants to choose a topic from the agenda (refer to Chapter 7) and focus their conversation on that point until they're ready to move on. This technique helps prevent them from jumping around from topic to topic.

- ✔ **Remember that any idea is a good idea:** Brainstorming is about articulating any and all possibilities before deciding on anything.

- ✔ **Follow time limits:** Some of the best ideas come when people are pressed for time. Keep the brainstorming short, and then spend quality time refining the ideas.

✔ **Say then weigh:** Generate as many ideas as possible before weighing and evaluating a single one. Don't let the brainstorming process derail by getting bogged down in the details. I like to capture the first few ideas and then start saying 'and' after every suggestion. Keep the ideas coming!

✔ **Create a parking lot:** If one of the parties has an idea for a different agenda item, quickly jot it down next to that topic (I call that 'parking it') until you're ready to move to that point. Similarly, if the employees think of something they need to check out or want to add another topic for discussion, into the parking lot it goes.

Narrowing the possible solutions

After the employees generate a number of ideas, start making some decisions. Help them establish evaluation criteria for their proposals and determine how best to choose agreements that meet both of their needs. Such criteria are typically related to common values, or expectations and guidelines set forth by your workplace.

Ask questions that address the benefits and limitations of each proposed solution. Specifically:

✔ What do each of you like about this proposal? What don't you like about it?

✔ How might the idea be improved?

✔ Does it meet the needs you both stated as being important? If not, what can be changed for it to do so?

Asking Great Questions

Good questions are the primary tools of a skilled mediator. Asking questions allows you to gather information, expand your employees' perspectives, generate options and orient your process to the future. Additionally, good questions help you reinforce that this conversation is a dialogue, not a monologue (no lengthy speeches!).

The following sections cover the different types of questions you can ask, the order in which you should ask them, and the kinds of questions you should avoid.

Knowing which questions to use when

Different types of questions accomplish different tasks. The trick is knowing which questions to ask and what kind of response each type generates.

Closed-ended questions

Closed-ended questions require a specific and direct answer to a specific and direct question. The answer is often implied by the question itself. You may think of closed-ended questions as those that only elicit a yes or no answer. This is true to some extent, but they can be very useful when trying to help your employees sort through and narrow down a number of options.

Here's an example of a closed-ended question you would frame after hearing a few proposals: 'If your options are to continue working on this program with William or begin a new program from scratch, which option best meets your needs and the needs of the company?'

Use these questions to clarify a situation with employees in order to develop a common understanding, or to call attention to a situation that you believe needs some action or further steps. For example: 'Is this the kind of communication the two of you typically use together? Is it working for you? Would you be willing to try something different?'

Open-ended questions

Where closed-ended questions can give you specific information and can help narrow down choices, *open-ended questions* give so much more. These questions are designed to widen your discussion and invite your employees to participate in a dialogue. For example: 'What possibilities do you see? What solutions can you imagine that would work for both of you?'

These questions don't presume any answers. They do, however, require more nuanced and thoughtful responses than just yes or no. In fact, they encourage the listener to look toward the future and consider potential solutions for the problem. They also open doors and expand the conversation in ways that you never expect, because they invite listeners to provide more information and expand their thoughts.

These questions leave open the possibility that your employees can take their thoughts almost anywhere, which is usually where you need them to go. Keep a couple of questions in your back pocket and come prepared to ask questions that give everyone a broader view of the situation.

Sequencing your questions

People in conflict can have a hard time getting out of a circular conversation mode. In addition to their emotional attachment to issues, their problems stem from the fact that they can't stay focused on one thing before moving onto another.

Use your power as the facilitator to change the circular conversation by sequencing your questions. Each question you ask should follow from the answer to the previous question. Help the parties fully explore the topics of discussion and truly flesh out the important ideas. Keep them on track and make sure they see you as being interested and invested in their discussion.

If your questions don't flow with the direction of the conversation, they can come off as jarring or abrupt, and your employees may lose momentum, or become confused about what you're asking. For example: 'What happened at the meeting that was difficult? Do the two of you use email or face-to-face discussions when you communicate? Who else do you think was affected by the argument?' These are all good questions, but if you put them one after another, you make it difficult to explore any one area of concern.

Sequence questions follow thoughts in such a way that each one follows directly from the answer to the previous question. Here's an example:

> **You:** What is most important for you to accomplish today?
>
> **Your employee:** I just want to have a professional working relationship with Angela.
>
> **You:** Tell me about that. What does a professional working relationship look like to you?
>
> **Your employee:** I guess I just want the gossip to stop. I'm sick of listening to her talk about everyone else's business and creating drama.

You: You'd like to limit your conversations to work-related activities. How do you think the two of you can create that?

In addition to being sequenced, questions like these follow a subtle path by moving people from identifying values to describing and defining them to designing a path to achieve them. In this way, you can move employees who are stuck arguing about what has happened and who's at fault to working together to create a plan for the future.

You can word great sequenced questions any number of ways, but you should often follow a very basic pattern:

- ✔ What is it that's most important to you? (Name values)

- ✔ What does it look like? (Describe values)

- ✔ How do you get there? (Brainstorm solutions)

Avoiding unproductive questions

Some questions can bring the meeting to a screeching halt or, at the very least, make it difficult for your employees to work constructively. Good questions expand, explore and create, while unproductive questions tend to minimise, limit and place blame. I recommend avoiding the following types of questions.

Leading questions

Simply put, *leading questions* are your answers with a question mark tacked on to the end for good measure. Often, people ask these questions with the best of intentions, trying to provide insight or options but, in actuality, leading questions limit the creativity and ability of your employees to come up with their own solutions. Some examples:

- ✔ Have you ever considered getting some training in the new software?

- ✔ Can you think of any reason you wouldn't want to share resources with Bill?

- ✔ Couldn't you come in at another time and take care of the paperwork then?

Assumptive questions

Assumptive questions assume that the answer to the question is obvious. In addition to being limiting and closed-ended, they tend to create negative reactions in listeners and usually shut down the conversation, rather than expanding it. For example:

- ✔ You realise your actions make you look really unprofessional, right?
- ✔ Don't you want to have a successful career here?

Why questions

Questions that begin with the word *why* rarely give you anything from the listener other than defensiveness. And with good reason! Essentially, you've asked the listener to defend the position he holds or the actions he has taken, rather than discussing what's important to him about the positions and actions. *Why* questions don't allow for an answer that provides much of anything except for excuses and defensiveness, and they often elicit nothing more than an 'I don't know' from the listener. Plus, they run the risk of making people feel like kindergarteners being scolded by the principal. For example:

- ✔ Why did you write that email to accounting?
- ✔ Why didn't you call Christina to tell her about the change to the staff meeting?
- ✔ Why did you think Reece would be okay with that?

With the right inquisitive tone, some why questions may be okay (especially in private meetings, like those I describe later in this chapter). But instead of fretting whether you've mastered the correct tone, you can simply use an imperative statement if you think finding out why an employee did what she did will help you understand her perspective: 'Tell me about the email to accounting.'

Working through Resistance

No magic formula exists for moving through resistance. Every one of your employees is unique and carries his own experiences, personalities and core values. And because each person comes to this conversation with different needs, each one will likely respond differently to different techniques.

Your goal is *not* to bully your employees into working through resistance. You have a lot of power in your role, and if you use it to force your employees to find a solution, they may not arrive at an appropriate or sustainable answer.

In the following sections, I reveal some of the causes of resistance and give you strategies you can use to overcome it.

Identifying common causes of resistance

Before you address how (or even if) you want to work through resistance, have a sense of where it's coming from. Take a look at some of the common causes of resistance to discussions:

✔ **Strong emotion:** The parties involved are either stuck in the past, reacting to each other's actions or language, or are unable to hear what each other is saying. Strong emotions tend to limit people's ability to think critically and can hamper progress.

✔ **Distrust:** Your employees may not trust each other to keep the conversation civil and on track, or they may not trust your process. This can be because of their work history, their relationship, bad experiences or even threats, both real and perceived. They may not trust you, either, as a neutral facilitator. Don't take it personally — do your best to prove them wrong.

✔ **Failure to communicate/listen:** Lack of communication may happen because employees simply have different communication styles, or it may happen because they choose hostile or unproductive language. An employee may use specific body language to indicate that she can't (or won't) listen to what the other has to say, such as turning her back while the other is speaking, crossing her arms and refusing to make eye contact, or even putting her hands over her ears (yes, that has actually happened!).

✔ **Failure to see options:** An employee may come to the meeting with only one idea in mind, and it usually involves never having to see or work with the other person again. Mediation meetings work best when a plethora of ideas are on the table; a narrow view of solutions certainly slows down the progress.

✔ **Overconfidence/moral high ground:** If an employee believes, justly or not, that he's in the right and that he has been wronged, he may be overconfident in his position. He may think his position is stronger than it is, because others in the workplace may have sided with him. You'll often hear an employee in this state of mind say that he 'just wants to do what's right for the company'. Parties who take this stance are reluctant to negotiate because they believe their power comes from being justified in their position.

✔ **Negative association:** Essentially, an employee may choose not to negotiate or accept offers simply because it's the other person who proposed the solution. A suggestion or offer that would be perfectly reasonable if proffered by anyone else is regarded as not good enough, based entirely on the messenger.

With all the things that can cause people not to want to negotiate, you may be thinking, how on earth do people ever get past this part? It takes some work and some attention, but you can do a number of things when you reach an impasse. Read on for those ideas.

Exploring the impasse

To help your employees see the conflict that brought them to the table with a new set of eyes, start by asking each of them to describe the stalemate. They may find that they're stuck for very different reasons, and they may discover some workarounds for the areas where they can find commonality.

You may want to ask them to describe each other's position or concerns, which helps them see beyond their own view. Do this carefully, however, as you don't want them to mischaracterise the other's position, or downplay the significance of the other's view.

Creating options

If your employees are stuck repeatedly talking about the details of the problems they face, encourage them to focus on potential solutions instead. This seems like a no-brainer, doesn't it? But don't be surprised when the conversation turns into a rehashing of all the difficulties.

Help them brainstorm answers rather than dwell on problems. You can accomplish this by turning their attention away from the past and focusing instead on the future. Your questions should be future-focused, opening conversations around what *could be* rather than what *has been*. Ask things like:

- ✔ If the issues were solved today and it's three weeks down the road, can you describe how you see the project being completed?

- ✔ What new possibilities might come from working this out?

- ✔ How would each of you like to see the schedule assigned for the next month?

Encourage both people to attempt a form of detached brainstorming. In other words, get them thinking about what others might do in a similar situation, rather than what they are doing. This kind of brainstorming isn't limited by what they think they know about each other, so it's easier for them to respond. I often ask the parties to share any ideas they'd give Joe in accounting if he were to describe this conflict to them.

Testing the margins

Create clarity around the boundaries of the situation by asking the parties to give some thought to their other options. Ask if they've considered what happens next if they're unable to reach an agreement. Are they comfortable moving forward without a solution? Your questions should help your employees consider the impact and the implications of not moving forward. (For more tips on troubleshooting problem areas, see Chapter 9.) Similarly, encourage both to describe the best and worst solutions that *could* come out of their meeting. Perhaps they'll be able to find some daylight between the ideal and not-so-ideal agreements.

After they give descriptions of the best and worst outcomes, discuss what they see as the best and worst results of ending the meeting without agreements in place. If they're unable to come up with a solution during the meeting and they choose to walk away, what's next for them? You may know the answer to that question already, but ask it anyway.

Refocusing on values

Mediations rely heavily on dialogue that's centred on the employees' core values and the positions they've taken. Your employees have likely gotten off track, or maybe they're having a difficult time articulating the points that are so important to them. Help by really focusing the conversation on the critical elements.

Ask them to describe what values their proposals address. I like to ask questions such as

- ✔ What does each of your proposals give you? How do they each meet your own needs? How do they meet the other person's needs?

- ✔ How do your proposals satisfy the values that each of you has identified as important?

If you've gone through this exercise and still find that they're struggling, ask them to mentally step away from the negotiation and to describe the qualities of a good agreement instead. Whatever their answers, ask if any of the ideas they've thrown out so far match the good agreement criteria. If the answer is no, encourage them to create new proposals that include the qualities that each of them just described.

Interrupting negative behaviours

Don't be surprised if the parties have difficulty working within the boundaries of behaviour you've set out for them (refer to Chapter 7). Meetings like these can create a lot of anxiety and tension, and in the face of difficult conflict, even the most level-headed person can lose her cool. However, you don't want those moments to impede your discussion, so address them when you see them.

If someone is continually using language that isn't helpful, you can ask him to

- ✔ Use different words

- ✔ Reframe his statements in more neutral terms

- ✔ Speak in 'I-statements'

- ✔ Summarise in terms that the other person can more easily understand

Some topics and conversations cause physical reactions like clenched jaws and rolling eyes. If this happens, call it out when you see it. When it catches my attention, I sometimes say, 'I notice that when John said *xyz*, you had a reaction. Tell me about that.'

Don't be afraid to address negative behaviour. If it's affecting your conversation, it won't likely go away without assistance. And if you've noticed it, you can bet big money that the other party has noticed it as well.

Another option is to take a break and meet with each of your employees separately. Check out the section 'Meeting Privately with Each Individual' for the ins and outs of a successful confidential discussion.

Trying one last time to overcome resistance

A time may come when you realise that, no matter how hard you've tried, your employees are unable to resolve their problems with you as the facilitator. When this happens, your participants probably already know it and are prepared to move on to the next step, whatever that may be. But you may not be finished just yet. Your employees may attempt to make a last-ditch effort to solve the problem if they know you've reached the end of your line. So as you're wrapping up, ask whether they have any last (or even best) offers before you end the discussion. This gives them an opportunity to share any last-minute goodies they may have been holding onto, and it can be exactly what you need to finally get the breakthrough you've been looking for.

Meeting Privately with Each Individual

At some point in the mediation meeting, you may get the sense that one of the parties would like an opportunity to brainstorm or test assumptions with you without fear of reprisal. Maybe the emotions that both employees have been expressing are threatening to overtake the process, or maybe the employees simply need a breather.

Whatever the case, a private meeting is an excellent opportunity for you to provide a different venue for participants to discuss the conflict on a different level. If you opt to call a private meeting, you need to decide how to break, whom to meet with first and what kind of approach to take in the private meeting. I cover all these topics in the following sections.

Be sure your employees understand that they aren't in trouble and that you haven't given up on the conversation. Explain that you think this is a good opportunity to take a quick break and try something new. Framing this meeting as a positive step in your process helps you manage your employees' reactions.

Choosing who goes first

No hard and fast rule exists about how to decide whom to meet with first. You know your employees, and you're the best person to make an assessment about what to do, but here are some determining factors that can help you:

- ✔ **Assess emotions:** Is one of the people decidedly more emotional than the other? Or is one struggling more because of the emotional climate? Decide whether meeting with this person first is an opportunity to help her vent and process, or if letting her relax alone for a few minutes while you meet with the other person is the best use of time.

- ✔ **Assess power:** For this conversation to be successful, you want power to be roughly in balance between your participants. An employee who says he doesn't care, is too overwhelmed to speak, or can't act in his own best interests may be telling you that he feels disempowered. Meeting first with an employee who feels powerless will probably be more effective than trying to squelch or minimise the other employee's power.

- ✔ **Assess behaviour:** Is one of your employees acting out of character? Do you see a typically soft-spoken employee becoming aggressive and demeaning, or an outspoken employee suddenly not making a peep? If so, something has changed, and you need to check it out.

Whomever you choose to meet with first, be sure to clarify to the other person that she'll have the same opportunity as the first person. Clarify, though, that equal *opportunity* doesn't necessarily mean equal *time*. Let both employees know that because you'll be meeting with both of them, going first doesn't really hold any benefit.

After you make your choice, give the employee that you aren't meeting with first something to do. I typically ask him to make a note of the agenda items and to brainstorm at least two new options or offers that have yet to be discussed. This assignment works more times than not. He'll likely labour to create something that works for both parties and come back with great solutions, and he may take great pride in pointing out the benefits to the other person.

Allowing parties to open up with added confidentiality

When you send one of your employees out of the room so you can continue your conversation with the other, make a quick statement clarifying that during this time, you're applying an additional layer of confidentiality. What this means, essentially, is that anything she shares with you during this time you won't bring up with the other employee in his private meeting or during an open session. That means you won't do so *even if she asks you to*. This is an important convention, because it

✔ Requires employees to take ownership of any solutions they generate and reinforces your role as a facilitator, rather than an adjudicator.

✔ Allows employees the freedom to create and explore without fear of reprisal from the other party.

✔ Gives employees the opportunity to save face if they need to discuss items that are uncomfortable or potentially embarrassing.

✔ Allows you to discuss topics in such a way that prepares the employee to handle how to share information with the other employee when both return to the open session.

Venting and exploring

One of the most vital things you do during a private meeting is create a safe and open environment for your employee. You may likely see this as an opportunity to get down to the bottom of things, but you won't be able to accomplish that unless your employee trusts that this is a safe place to have that conversation.

Begin the conversation in the same way for each participant by asking, 'How is this going for you?' Inquire about his experiences, thoughts and ideas, and encourage him to share any of his reactions to the process. Don't spend any time trying to address specific conflict business yet, because he probably isn't ready to go there. Initially, spend some time reflecting emotions, validating concerns and summarising positions. For more information on these skills, refer to Chapter 7.

As your conversation develops, keep these concepts in mind:

- ✔ **Explore values:** Ask him to describe not only his own values, but also what he believes the other employee values (this is key for him to see the other person's point of view!). Ask him to explain how the values play out in the workplace and in his relationship with the other party. Doing this helps him generate proposals that are based in values, which are the most satisfying in the long run.

- ✔ **Identify common ground:** Anytime you can encourage an employee to identify what he has in common with a co-worker, you're helping him create opportunities for solutions. Common ground bridges the gap between different experiences, perspectives, values and ideas.

- ✔ **Ask about the other person:** When you hear the employee make negative comments about the other person — and you will — ask questions that move him from thinking about his own perspective to that of the other person's. For example, if Roger says Jeanne owes him an apology, ask, 'What do you think is preventing her from offering an apology? Do you think she might need to hear anything from you in order to get that?'

- ✔ **Brainstorm options:** Encourage him to think about creative solutions, without limits. You'll be able to reality test later, but by giving him license to think outside the box, he may find solutions that he never imagined possible.

- ✔ **Develop proposals:** Asking future-oriented and other brainstorming questions will help him develop potential offers and solutions. Especially when he seems stuck in what he doesn't like or want, encourage him to speak about what he'd like or want instead.

✔ **Conduct a reality test:** After you have a few proposals developed, help him sort through and test each one for any potential problems. You may also need to reality test with employees who are unable to come up with solutions. By addressing what will happen if he leaves without a solution, you may help him find inspiration and language to create proposals.

Preparing an employee to return to the open session

Forming proposals privately is really only half the battle. Now your employee needs to ask his co-worker to accept the proposal, which may be difficult, considering that they've struggled with their communication in the past. You can help him by letting him practise the proposal, with you acting as the co-worker.

Instead of commenting on whether the proposal sounds good or bad, ask him some specific feedback questions:

✔ How did that sound to you?

✔ How do you think [the other employee] will respond to it?

✔ If you were [the co-worker], how would you like to hear such a proposal offered?

✔ Do you think you could frame your idea in any other way?

 Get a commitment from him that he will, in fact, make these proposals when both parties return to the open session with you. It does you no good to have spent the time in your private session if he has no intention of making the offer or asking for things he wants. Ask him if he's comfortable sharing his proposals and, if so, ask him to jot them down before he leaves the room.

Back in the open session, employees may forget what they wanted to say (and you can't help because you've promised confidentiality), so having it in front of them gives a visual cue and keeps the conversation going.

Chapter 9

Offering Proposals and Crafting Agreements

- -

In This Chapter

▶ Reconvening a mediation session

▶ Creating settlements

▶ Closing the meeting on a positive note

- -

*Y*ou're ready to continue your open session discussion with the two employees engaged in this conflict. Your hope is that the continued discussion will lead to proposed solutions and an agreement that settles the conflict.

In this chapter, I show you how to make room for quality communication, acknowledge new perspectives and encourage your employees to have a positive outlook on their future working relationship — which inevitably will include some conflict. You also find tips on how to give your staff the hope they need beyond the meeting to know they can address future problems and not just solve this one issue in a vacuum. Finally, I tell you the six non-negotiable attributes of a solid agreement.

Continuing Negotiations

As you prepare to continue negotiations, know that your employees' communication improving is more important than coming to consensus right away. As their manager, you may be itching for them to give each other some sort of agreement that you can document but, at this point, you just have to trust that good agreements will come from good communication.

In this section, I tell you how to start this part of the conflict resolution process, and I tell you what to listen for as your employees continue their discussion.

Proceeding with the meeting

If you met privately with each employee engaged in this conflict (refer to Chapter 8 for details), continue the negotiations by bringing them back to the room in which you first met (refer to Chapter 7 for more about the initial meeting). Start this part of the mediation process off right: Commend your participants for the work they've done so far.

This process can be challenging, and can tax even the most energetic person's reserves. A quick observation from you that their hard work is recognised can go a long way toward reenergising your employees — and it may even give them just enough oomph to get over the hump. In fact, it's a good idea to praise good work and progress at any stage of the meeting.

Remind the parties that your private meetings were confidential and that you won't bring up anything they shared with you during those meetings. Encourage your employees to think back to their private meetings and decide if they discussed anything that either of them would like to share — this strategy reinforces the responsibility that each employee has for speaking on his own behalf, and puts each employee firmly in the driver's seat.

Don't be surprised if you see some hesitation. Your employees may go through a brief period of 'I don't want to be the first to speak'. Especially when they feel uncertain or distrustful, they may want to wait to hear what the other is thinking before they're willing to give voice to their own thoughts. The important thing to remember is not to rescue them from this uncertainty. Be prepared to push yourself away from the table and wait — and sometimes wait and wait! This approach always works for me, and I recommend you try it yourself.

You may be tempted to think that silence between your employees is a sign that things aren't working well, but try seeing silence as a tool you can use to your (and their) benefit. Silence is a void that wants to be filled. The more patient you are, and the more comfortable you appear in it, the more likely one of them is to fill that void. Lean back in your seat or pull away from the table as an indication that you won't be filling

Give the participants a chance to digest and then speak about what they've heard. For example, I may say, 'Ron, I can see that the information Anita provided us about the amount of time she's spent on this project outside of work is new information to you. Can you tell us what you think about that?'

Acknowledgements

Sometimes, an employee may make observations or statements of genuine appreciation for the other person or acknowledge something important to her. However, because of the nature of these conversations, acknowledgments can be either glossed over or completely lost in the mix.

You're in a good position to make sure that important points *don't* get missed. When you hear a game changer that gets lost along the way, jump in and clarify it for your parties. For example, you may say, 'Shannon, I just heard you say that though the two of you disagree about the conclusions drawn from your data, you were, in fact, impressed with Sarah's writing on her quarterly report. Sarah, did you hear that as well?'

Changes in perspective or tone

When an employee has a chance to vent with you privately and explore new ideas and possibilities, he may return to negotiations with a renewed sense of purpose and a new commitment to solving problems. A lot of good work can get done in these situations, so be sure to make a note of this change when you see it! Your employees will appreciate the pat on the back, but your encouragement also helps cement this new way of solving problems.

Note changes in communication patterns, posture, willingness to give each other the benefit of the doubt, and any number of things that may be different from their initial attitudes toward each other. I make note of these in the following way: 'Wow, Eamon and Audrey, I notice a real change from earlier in this meeting. I think the two of you are working really well together. I commend you for that. Keep up the good work.'

Apologies

Some of the best moments in mediation take place in the form of sincere apologies. These moments don't always happen, and a lack of apologies doesn't say anything about your skill as a mediator, but when any apology does happen, it can literally change everything.

that gap. Sooner or later, one of your employees will star\
talking.

One caveat: You'll likely know from your private meetings
whether offers or proposals are forthcoming. If that's the
case, allow some time for these offers to come to the surfac
If offers aren't forthcoming, long periods of silence may only
make matters worse. As long as your employees appear to b
considering their options or weighing their proposals, give th
the time and space to create them. If they aren't engaged in tl
process, remind them of any proposals that were on the table
remind them of items left on the agenda, recap common groun
or ask whether either of them wants to revisit any points you
discussed earlier.

Listening for the good stuff

Pay attention to what each employee is saying because a lot
of good work happens after your private meetings, but it's not
always going to be couched in really good language. So listen for
it yourself.

If your employees come back from their private meetings and
they're doing well and negotiating, stay out of their way. Let
them do the work, and make note of the things you're hearing,
so you can start transitioning them into the 'settlement' phase of
your conversation when the time is right. (See the later section
'Developing Solutions during the Open Session' for more details
on the settlement phase of negotiations.)

But if one party is saying something worth noting, help her
out by stopping the conversation and pointing it out to the
other person so he can acknowledge it or respond. Be sure that
none of the important points is lost along the way. Do some
summarising any time you hear any of the following.

New information

Often, the conflict that your employees have been experiencing
hinges on information that one party may not have had full
access to. And, in many cases, when this new information
comes to light, your employees may need a moment to consider
what's being shared. This new information may change their
perspective on the other person, may shed new light on
decisions that were made and may even affect offers on the table
(or proposals that have yet to be made!).

If you know someone wants to apologise because she shared that information with you privately (refer to Chapter 8 for tips on productive private meetings), coach her to deliver a three-part apology that includes

- ✓ I-statements, as in, 'I'm sorry that I ... ,' not 'I'm sorry that you ...'

- ✓ An assurance that it won't happen again

- ✓ A sincere request for instruction on how to make up for it

Without all three parts (and the right tone of voice and eye contact, of course), it's difficult for people to receive an apology as the conclusion of an act or event. Putting the three together sounds like this, 'I'm sorry I approached you about the reports in front of everyone in the meeting. You have my word that it won't happen again. What can I do to make up for my poor behaviour?' It doesn't sound like this, 'I'm sorry you took what I did the wrong way and got so mad. You know I didn't mean it, so let's just get past this thing, okay?'

 Apologies can get lost in the mix of a conflict conversation. A participant can easily tuck an apology into the middle of another statement he's making, minimising the impact. Or he may share it in an awkward way, trying to save face. Or it could simply be that the apology isn't framed in a way that's easily heard by the other person.

If you hear an apology shared and it's missed by the other party, make sure you draw attention to it: 'Becky, before you move on, I just want to make sure that this doesn't get missed. I think I heard Denise apologise for the way you were treated when you visited the shipping department. Did you hear that as well?'

Unfortunately, sometimes when apologies are expressed, they're understood but not accepted. The other party not accepting an apology that's been offered doesn't have to be the end of your conversation, but it may require some work on your part. Acknowledge both parties and summarise their feelings about the apology itself. Ask some questions about whether the apology could be accepted at another time and, if so, what it would take to get to that place: 'Anne, I want to acknowledge that you've offered an apology to Owen. And Owen, for you, I hear that at this time you're unable to accept it. I'm wondering if you can imagine a time when you might be able to accept such an apology and what it might take for you to be able to do that?'

When sincere apologies are made and accepted, the air in the room changes. Your employees' body language will open up, they'll sit up straighter, and the tense muscles in their faces and necks will soften. These are signs you're on the right track.

Proposals

Often, by the time you reach this part of a mediation, your employees are ready to start making proposals to one another. Offers come in different forms, however, and some may be easier to pick up on than others. Consider the following:

- **Proposals may be clear and concise and offer little ambiguity as to the intent.** For example, one of your employees may say, 'I'd be willing to provide you a copy of the meeting notes on the days when you're unable to attend because of your other responsibilities.'

   If the other party continues to talk and doesn't respond, say: 'Maggie just made a specific proposal to you, Frank, to provide a copy of the meeting notes on the days when you're unable to attend. Does that work for you?'

- **Proposals may be more of a tit-for-tat.** This is where one employee is only willing to offer something if she's able to receive something as well. For example, an employee may say, 'I'd be happy to support the project plan among the rest of the team, but only if you send an email to the team first saying it was my idea and that we're working on it together.'

   If the other person doesn't automatically accept, say: 'Let's untangle Michael's proposal and approach one piece at a time. Gloria, how do you feel about sharing the collaboration efforts between you and Michael with the team?'

- **Proposals may be offered tentatively.** Or they may be offered in such a way that you may not be sure if they are, in fact, an offer at all. For example, an employee may say, 'Well, I guess I could take a look at restructuring the shift schedule, but I'm not sure if I'll be able to give you the times you're looking for.'

   Clarify proposals like this by saying, 'Brendon, are you proposing to Bill that you could take a look at restructuring the shift schedule? Could you tell him more about what you're thinking could happen with that so he can respond to a specific proposal?'

If your employees are doing well in this process, making offers and counteroffers, and if they seem to understand one another's perspectives and requests, take a more passive role. However, when you need to step in and summarise or follow up with clarifying questions, use clear language. Specifically, if you see your employees struggling to frame a proposal, step in and summarise what you've heard. Here are a couple of examples:

> Tony, it sounds as if you're willing to do some research on additional training options, but you're unsure whether that will answer Linda's request to broaden the scope of her job responsibilities. Did I get that right?

> Christina, I've heard you say that you'd like Scott to work harder when it's his day to stock the shelves. What does 'work harder' look like to you? What, specifically, would you like to propose he do?

Developing Solutions during the Open Session

As your employees' proposals begin to turn into agreements, you may be tempted to think that it's all downhill from here.

The truth is, even though you've spent a good amount of time and energy facilitating this conversation, and even though you and your employees are probably pretty exhausted because of the energy it takes to have this kind of meeting, you still have some work to do. In this section, I tell you how to pay attention to the details of proposals (ideas the parties have agreed to commit to) so you can reduce the probability that your employees will be back to mediate the exact same issue.

Recognising the non-negotiable elements of a good settlement

If you hear any proposed agreements, be sure to probe, prod and tweak them to make sure they're the best they can be. Good, solid agreements that satisfy everyone's needs and hold up over time don't just fall out of the sky. They have specific qualities that are important for you to look for in each of the proposals you discuss.

Think of this part of the mediated meeting as a litmus test to identify these particular attributes. If one of the following elements is missing, you increase the chances of the agreement falling apart and adding to the frustration of those involved. Give these elements proper consideration and you'll send the parties away with the greatest chance for success.

Doable

Agreements have to actually fit with reality. This attribute may sound obvious, but it's surprising how quickly unrealistic agreements can become part of a plan that sounds good on the surface but inevitably falls apart. When your employees begin to make agreements on the heels of a lengthy or difficult conflict, a lot of good energy can be generated. This is a good thing, and you want to tap into that energy, but don't be surprised when employees begin to agree to things that aren't doable because the two are on a roll or they're ready to agree to anything. Agreeing to something because it feels right in the moment can cause additional problems.

You know your organisation, so you should be able to gauge what you consider doable. If an agreement includes one one party coming in on a Saturday to complete his part of a project and the job site is shut down on weekends, the doable attribute can't be met.

Support the parties wherever you can but don't set them up for failure by allowing a creative solution you know won't fly with the rest of the company.

Specific

Clearly outline what each employee is agreeing to do. Additionally, ensure that agreements describe the steps that each person will take in order to accomplish tasks, in a way that leaves no ambiguity as to the expectations each has of the other.

Imagine two employees who decide that the best way to make sure that all the tasks assigned to them are getting fulfilled is to meet once a month for half an hour to discuss the workload. You can write it like this: 'Matt and Kate agree to meet once a month to discuss the workload.'

At the moment, Matt and Kate may think they have the exact same understanding of this meeting. But do they know when they're meeting? Are certain days or times better or worse for the discussion? For how long will they meet? And where will this meeting take place? How will they be sure that what needs to be discussed will get addressed? A better agreement looks more like this:

> Matt and Kate agree to meet at 10.30 am on the first Wednesday of every month, beginning next month, for a half-hour discussion in conference room A. This conversation will focus on making sure all the goals assigned to the training team are being met. Kate will bring a copy of the team's goal statement and a calendar to make a note of project deadlines. Matt will use the information to update the online team calendar by close of business that same day.

Durable

Although some agreements may only be intended to be short term or even one-time actions, agreements relating to ongoing relationships, processes and procedures should have a reasonably long shelf life.

If Tom agrees to stay late every Wednesday to tally the store receipts and you know he's going to start an evening course in a few weeks, will he be able to keep this agreement? Ask more questions and probe further if an agreement includes actions by either party that have the potential to cause an inconvenience or become tiring. Give both people permission to 'be real' about what they can commit to and ask them not to sign up for anything they feel they won't be able to sustain. Ask them to consider personal commitments, calendar commitments (like holidays), unpredictable factors (like traffic), and any possible organisational changes in the works.

Of course, you can't predict every unforeseen situation or event that could derail an agreement, but the more questions you ask — and have them answer — the more durable the agreement becomes. Give your staff permission to rework the agreement if it warrants a change down the road, and ask them to add language about any 'what ifs' they can foresee.

Balanced

Balanced agreements are not necessarily ones in which employees split their resources 50/50, or agree to do exactly half the work on a project they're assigned. Instead, balanced agreements show that both parties are willing to *give* something and *receive* something.

Even where one of your employees has decided to take the lion's share of the responsibility for resolving the problems at hand, look for ways to include the other employee in the process. This can be as simple as one employee agreeing to do a task, and the other employee agreeing to acknowledge him for it.

Balance in agreements goes hand in hand with the quality of _durability_ (refer to the preceding section for more on durability). This becomes evident after you've reached settlement and your parties have moved into implementing their agreements. If one employee looks back over the agreement down the road and feels as if the outcome was imbalanced, she may be less likely to honour her end of the arrangement, or she may even revisit the conflict anew.

Complete

Has everything of importance to the conflict been addressed by the agreements? If something was important to either party, address it in the agreement — even if the arrangement is to discuss it at a later date. Cover all the agenda items. (Check out the tips for building an effective meeting agenda in Chapter 7.) If it's on the agenda, make sure that you've addressed the issue in some way — either by documenting a solution, or by coming to some verbal agreement regarding how the parties intend to deal with it. If you don't make it through the list, note in the agreement that the parties didn't have a chance to discuss the item or were unable to come to agreement on it. This item will be a good starting point for any follow-up meetings.

Dot the _i_s and cross the _t_s. If either party starts to resist pinning down exact details, coach him by letting him know they'll both have a better chance at success if they take care of these details with you as a facilitator instead of walking away with a new misunderstanding to an old conflict.

Satisfying

Often, in the midst of conflict, employees express a concern that their agreements be _fair_. Let me encourage you instead, however, to support the idea that agreements be _satisfying_.

Look back on the rest of the meeting and note any values or interests that an employee shared with you, and ask her if the agreement meets those values. (For information on identifying values, refer to Chapter 2.) For example, if Curtis talked about his need for autonomy and the agreement doesn't mention

anything that delivers that to him on some level, it isn't
satisfying.

Troubleshooting problem areas

A number of factors can contribute to problems when you're
facilitating the solution/agreement portion of your mediation. Be
aware of these factors and pay attention to how they can affect
the overall quality of your process.

Vague language

Although using open-ended language is a good idea, when it's
time to write up agreements, be as clear and specific as you can
be. Avoid language that can be interpreted differently by the
parties, such as the following:

- As soon as possible
- If necessary
- Wherever appropriate
- When convenient
- More or less

Use language that almost feels like it's bordering on nitpicking.
Be specific! Use language such as the following:

- By (date and time)
- No later than
- Completed on
- Via company email

Settlement by attrition

Sometimes parties can begin to make agreements that they
don't necessarily intend to live up to. They may feel as if their
important issues haven't been addressed or that they lack the
power or the authority to effect a change. Don't let this happen!

When you hear language like 'I don't care — write down
whatever you want' or 'Let's just get it over with so we can
move on', pay attention. Your employee is telling you something.
Explore what's happening for him when you hear this kind of
language.

No settlement is better than a *bad* settlement. If a settlement is going to fall apart, better that it happen in the meeting where you can address the situation than after participants have left and returned to the workplace. Bad agreements can undermine trust in the process and adversely affect your employees.

Fatigue

Fatigue can greatly complicate a settlement. If employees are tired or worn down, they may be more likely to settle for an agreement that's incomplete or unrealistic, which places the likelihood of lasting satisfaction in jeopardy. Watch for signs that the participants are settling because they're exhausted and just want the process to come to an end. Don't let impatience move you too quickly through this part of the process. Take a break if necessary, but do make sure to take the time required to craft your agreements thoroughly.

I usually don't let mediations go for more than three hours before some sort of settlement writing begins, or I get an agreement to call a break with the intention of resuming the next day. You always have the option to schedule another meeting, so don't continue this one if the energy level is so low that productivity has waned.

Uncooperative behaviour

You're thinking that you're an amazing mediator because you've been able to guide your employees through a tough conversation that resulted in a list of agreements. Suddenly, one of your employees says she doesn't like the arrangements and starts talking in circles again. What just happened?! Truth is, this situation happens more times than I'd like, and here's why:

- **The employee never intended to come to agreement.** It's not unusual for an employee to come to a mediated meeting because he thinks he has to 'for the record'. He went through the motions, did what he suspected you wanted him to do, but didn't really negotiate in good faith. Try calling a private meeting to discuss the situation with him frankly and honestly. Create an atmosphere in which he feels comfortable telling you the truth.

- **The employee's needs haven't been met.** In one way or another, the agreement isn't meeting her needs or delivering what's most important to her. Hear her out a bit more, ask open-ended questions, and see whether you can help identify what's missing or has yet to be discussed.

✔ **Another plan is in play.** Sometimes, one of the people you're meeting with has something else in the works and isn't ready to spill the beans just yet. Maybe he's leaving the company, looking for a transfer to another department or seeking the advice of a third party. You may not be able to find out what's going on, but calling a private meeting for a candid conversation could help.

✔ **The employee just isn't ready.** Your employees will process conflict at different rates. Often, one of the employees isn't ready to let go of a grudge or doesn't yet trust that the future could be any different from the past. That's okay. Do what you can to let her talk, share her perspective with you and identify the issues. Consider arranging another meeting after she's had time to process a bit more.

Don't be fooled by a wolf in sheep's clothing! Any one of the preceding explanations for *not* signing an agreement can also be the reason an employee is ready to agree to and sign anything. Be especially wary of the 'yes man', who doesn't question, doesn't ask for anything in return and seems a little too eager to go along with everything his colleague wants. Chances are, either he's not going to sign the agreement or he has no intention of actually doing anything he's agreed to. Get to the bottom of his actions by calling a private meeting and exploring your concerns.

Incomplete contingency plans

Your employees may have the best of intentions and may have created a solid and complete agreement that they fully intend to live up to. However, even the best plans can fall apart if you don't address the 'what if' questions. Pay attention to all the possible areas that may cause an agreement to become invalid or would cause it to be renegotiated.

Look for any assumptions or expectations on which your employees are resting their agreements, and test what may happen if those assumptions are incorrect. Having a backup plan may seem redundant, and they may think it's overkill, but it benefits them greatly if and when things don't go according to plan.

Do a quick role-play in your mind: Imagine that two weeks have passed and your employees' agreements have fallen apart. What was the cause? What brought an otherwise solid agreement to a screeching halt? By considering the potential problems in this way, you may uncover some areas that need some additional attention.

One of the most common 'what ifs' that affects the success of agreements is the inclusion of third parties. If the person isn't in the room, she probably shouldn't be in the agreement. Agreements that are based on the actions of someone who hasn't had a chance to speak for herself often fall apart when that person is unwilling or unable to deliver on the agreement. Include language that takes the situation into account and makes room for adjustments, such as the following:

> Janet will ask Tom, by 5 pm on Wednesday the 3rd, if he is able to reset the start date of the marketing launch to the 30th. She will communicate Tom's response to Basma in person at the staff meeting. If Tom is unable to reset the start date, both parties agree to discuss the matter at a lunch meeting following the regular staff meeting and develop an alternative plan, which they will convey to the team via email on the 5th. Basma and Janet will write the email together and Basma will send it.

Writing it down

Although your participants may be communicating well in the moment, and seem to be on the same page when it comes to their expectations, you'll be amazed by how quickly they can come to very different conclusions after they leave the meeting.

Clearly spell out all the agreements in written form — not only to help your employees know that you expect them to honour the agreements they've made, but also to memorialise all the hard work they've done in the session. When writing the agreements, keep the following things in mind.

- ✔ **Use plain language.** Avoid using unnecessarily complex or legalistic-sounding jargon. Complex language only complicates your document and contributes to misunderstandings about content and context.

- ✔ **Address who, what, when, where and how.** Make sure that your employees can identify all the details for each of the points of their agreements. Specifically, consider who will be undertaking actions. What actions will they be performing? When and where will they be performed? How will the actions take place?

✔ **Remember confidentiality.** The intent of mediation is for everything that happens in the room to stay in the room. If others in the workplace know that the mediation is occurring, they may approach you or your participants for information. Encourage your participants to come up with a strategy for handling those requests, and consider including that strategy in the agreement. It may mean agreeing to simple, stock language like, 'Everything went well and we're happy with the outcome.' Encourage your employees to keep the mediation confidential and not include any specifics with co-workers or associates.

Sometimes after covering everything on the agenda, no specific agreements need to be documented. That doesn't mean, however, that you should simply send your employees out the door with a pat on the back. You may still want to make sure that your employees are on the same page and have come to some understanding about their situation.

Typically, such agreements are formulated when your employees have had a conversation about something intangible, have cleared up a misunderstanding or have a new way of approaching their work relationship. As long as you feel no details need to be captured to keep them on track, simply create a brief summary that they can take with them to remind them of their accomplishments.

Concluding the Meeting Optimistically

You can have a profound impact on your employees and workplace if you give your employees a chance to talk through their difficulties, provide an open atmosphere that encourages dialogue, and are interested in the continued stability and comfort of the work environment.

But not every mediated conversation ends on a triumphant note. In this section, I help you come up with a plan for dealing with all the possible outcomes.

Settlement

When things go smoothly, celebrate! And put your employees' efforts at the forefront. Let them know that you

✔ Appreciate their hard work

✔ Applaud their efforts

✔ Hope that their agreements will yield a stronger work dynamic for themselves and those they interact with on a daily basis

These conversations can dramatically change relationships. And when one relationship in your workplace changes for the better, it has the ability to radiate to the rest of the group.

Even when settlement doesn't produce a street party of good feelings, at the very least it can provide closure and a sense of relief. So, capitalise on whatever goodwill the settlements generate, and let your employees hear your appreciation. Wherever you can, offer your sincere praise of their work, and remind each person of the value and benefit in following through with his agreements. Tell both people that you want to assist them in following through with their agreements, and that if you can do anything to help them be more successful, you're available. Knowing they have you as a support in their ongoing work can help normalise and stabilise their commitment to making this agreement work.

Interim agreements

Not all agreements are fully realised and ready to become full-blown written settlements. In fact, sometimes writing a full agreement may be premature and can become a potential problem down the road. This is where interim agreements shine. Interim agreements are temporary in nature, such as trying out a new communication model for a period of time or adopting a new policy in the workplace and testing to see its effects.

When you help employees construct such an agreement, both people should understand that it's for a *specific amount of time*. Be sure that they're clear about how long this agreement will last, how they'll know it's time to re-evaluate, and when they'll address the outcomes of the interim agreement.

Taking one step at a time with agreements is not a negative reflection of your abilities as a facilitator or manager. You want to set up your staff for success, so let them try things on for a while, discover what works and what doesn't work, and then retool the agreement. Let them know that it's better to have something that works for both parties than a promise neither of them can keep.

No settlement

No matter how hard they try, your employees may be unable to come to a solution. Impasse happens even when employees have the best of intentions and you're relying on a strong process and skill set. Your employees (and even you) may leave frustrated and disheartened.

As long as you've stuck to the process, asked good questions, and encouraged the co-workers to talk with one another, you've done all that you can. The process belongs to you, but the solution belongs to your employees. Yet, it's frustrating to know that you've done everything in your power and still found a roadblock at the end of the trail.

As you bring your process to a close, try the following to help bring closure to the discussion:

✔ **End on a positive note.** Even though they may not have reached any agreements, look for anything that you can highlight as a positive outcome. Even something as simple as validating that each employee shared her perspective — and heard what the other had to say — can help them feel as if the meeting wasn't a waste.

✔ **Discuss next steps.** Clearly outline what their options are after they (or you) have decided that mediation isn't going to be a good solution for them. Helping your parties have a clear picture of other avenues for resolving this issue can help them leave with some sense of closure. This may be where you offer to bring in an outside mediator or counsellor, or talk about what other resources are available in the company. Feel free to ask them what they feel their next steps are. That question often brings out important details for both to consider and may bring them back to the table for another discussion.

✔ **Don't close the door.** While closing up shop, mention that this is not their one and only chance at a solution. Inform them that, although now may not be the best time for mediation, they're always welcome to return if they want to give it another shot. One of the employees may have a change of heart after he's had time to consider something that you or his co-worker said in the meeting.

Chapter 10

Adapting a Conflict Meeting for the Entire Team

*W*hen a conflict gets to the point that it's affecting an entire team or department, including as many people as possible in resolution efforts is often necessary and even beneficial. This chapter helps you refine your role as a meeting facilitator, walks you through organising a meeting and focuses on the art of working with a large group.

Acting as Facilitator

Even if employees or colleagues have viewed you as the problem-solver or go-to person in the past, when you're in a group meeting to address conflict, you take on a different function — that of neutral facilitator. So this isn't the time to deliver a lecture, stifle comments or questions, and then send staff back to work with their tail between their legs. Rather, you want to create an environment in which the attendees work through problems and build their own solutions. You're the (somewhat) objective guide at this point.

As facilitator, you need to communicate that the meeting is a safe and positive place where the team is allowed to communicate openly, share perspectives and work through ideas together. Focus your efforts on the process (how) and the content (what), as follows:

- ✔ **Process:** The process is the infrastructure that creates an atmosphere in which participants effectively work together, knowing that each person has a reasonable chance to express her views and that these views won't be ignored or tossed aside. Process elements include

  - Involving participants

  - Managing communication

  - Building trust

  - Giving support to group members

  - Generating ideas and evaluation strategies

  - Administering procedures for decision-making, taking action and moving to next steps

- ✔ **Content:** The content is everything from what group members are discussing to the quality and quantity of the ideas they're sharing. Before the meeting, use content to form a plan. Afterward, use it to move forward with resolution. Examples of content include

  - The ideas being generated

  - The issues to be discussed

  - The decisions being made

  - The plan being developed

  - The steps taken to carry out the plan

  - The progress to be reviewed

Gathering Information from the Group

If you're considering a team meeting to address a conflict, you need to build on what you already know so that you can assess and understand the needs and status of the group more fully.

In this section, I discuss a variety of techniques you can use to gather information from as many of the team members as possible, because the more you know, the better your meeting will be.

Recognising what you know

Before you jump in and start exploring the situation with other people, spend some time contemplating a few things on your own. Ask yourself:

- ✔ What are my observations of the team dynamics at this point?

- ✔ What issues have been brought to my attention?

- ✔ Can I identify themes from these concerns and complaints?

- ✔ Is the intensity between team members increasing?

You can then use what you know as a jumping off point to find out what you don't know.

Crafting questions to find out more

Formulating good questions helps you gain more than the basic information. Good questions are open-ended, yet still have some structure. Consider these two questions:

> Example #1: How do you feel?

> Example #2: How has this incident affected you?

Example #1 is too open and lacks connection to the subject. Example #2 links the question to the situation at hand and allows the participant to answer with how he feels and what he thinks. Your goal is to allow the participants to feel free to share what's most important to them in a way that provides solid, valuable information that you can work from.

Another way to ask questions is to order them in a past-present-future structure. This allows people to move along a natural path from what has occurred to what's happening now to what the situation could be moving forward. I often use questions like these:

- ✔ **Past:**
  - • When did the conflict begin for you?
  - • What incidents have occurred?
  - • What impact has this conflict had on you?

- What steps have you taken to resolve the conflict?
- What effect, if any, did those steps have?

✔ **Present:**

- What would you like to see changed?
- What ideas do you have?
- Are you aware of any external pressures that are affecting the group?

✔ **Future:**

- What do you want to see happen?
- What would be the best outcome for the team?
- What will you need so that you can work well in the future?

After you ask questions about the conflict, make sure to include some other questions that help people focus on the positive qualities of the group and set the tone for a productive team conversation. Consider these:

✔ What do you feel are the strengths and greatest successes of this group?

✔ What are you most proud of in this group?

✔ What is your vision of what this group can be in the future?

For other tips on asking questions, refer to Chapter 8.

Using interviews and surveys

You can use multiple methods for gathering information from a group. Whether you choose to use individual interviews, group interviews or surveys depends on the group's size, the need for personal connection, the conflict's intensity and time constraints. If you have a large group with varying job responsibilities, interview members in each department to gather team and individual feedback on how a change will affect these groups as a whole. If you have a time constraint that doesn't allow for multiple group discussions and you trust that one person can speak for many, interview a representative from each group.

Interviews

If you have a group of ten or fewer, take the time to speak to each party privately by personal interview or phone conversation. One-on-one conversations build trust and help each person feel comfortable when it's time to move into the larger group discussion. Private interviews also give you an opportunity to coach participants on how to share their perspective and insight with others.

Schedule all the appointments prior to starting. This gives everyone a chance to prepare and gives you time between interviews to summarise the information you elicit. Make sure to schedule each interview for the same duration — about 30 minutes — but realise that some will run short and others will run long.

Surveys

Gathering feedback by way of a written or online survey — or questionnaire — is an effective choice when the group is large, when safety and anonymity are desired or when people are in distant locations.

You get more truthful answers when you allow survey participants to respond to questions anonymously. Be upfront about the purpose and use of the survey and whether it will be kept confidential.

Good questionnaires have well-defined goals with clear and concise sentences. Questions should be simple and to the point to reduce misunderstanding. Customise your survey to provide as much information as you need to feel comfortable evaluating the issues, but be succinct. No-one wants to spend hours on these things!

If you'd rather not tackle putting your own questionnaire together, a number of online services can help you, such as Survey Monkey or PeoplePulse. Some of these services are free, though most offer advanced options for a one-time fee or a subscription-based payment schedule. These services allow you to customise professionally designed templates with your own questions that you can email to your participants, or link to a website that administers the survey for you.

Creating a timeline

Create a timeline of events or incidents with the information you gather. This helps you understand more completely what key events happened, when they took place and their impact on specific employees. This information allows you to build an agenda for the group meeting that addresses both broad perspectives and specific issues.

By creating a timeline and conducting interviews to pinpoint the beginning and middle of the conflict, you can build a group meeting agenda that focuses on the exact moments that teamwork fractured, which makes for a much more productive discussion.

Assessing the Intensity of a Conflict

Assessing the intensity and level of emotion in a conflict helps you determine how and when to proceed. If tension is growing and people are beginning to take sides, or if conversations that were occurring in private are now flowing into public areas, the intensity is increasing and you need to act. (For more information on emotional intensity and when to respond, refer to Chapter 2.)

If the team members are having disagreements but are still using language that includes the word 'we', and they're open to brainstorming solutions, the group meeting would include the group's participation in identifying problem areas and issues as well as ownership in the solutions.

If, on the other end of the scale, full-blown warfare has erupted, you're likely to hear evasive 'he/she/they' language and have staff member who are closed to listening and are using aggressive and negative language. In this situation, consider a series of shorter meetings in which you solely identify the goal for the discussion and draw out what team members believe they need to discuss in a longer meeting.

For example, if a team is experiencing a complex problem, you may call one meeting to focus only on administrative policies, a second that looks at customer service and a third for communication options. These brief, focused meetings, where only topics are discussed (without getting into the details behind the topics), help your team become aware of what the issues are for everyone involved, and so can help build a new team dynamic. You may also consider using smaller groups to create safety and bring out concerns more effectively.

Formulating a Meeting Plan

When you're facing a group conflict, the more upfront planning you do, the better your odds are for a fruitful outcome, so set yourself up for success. Prior to the meeting, do the following:

- ✔ Create a goal statement.

- ✔ Set an agenda and plan meeting logistics (time, place).

- ✔ Engineer ground rules.

- ✔ Assign tasks if you plan to use additional facilitators.

- ✔ Identify and collect data, charts, reports and so on.

- ✔ Clarify time constraints and deadlines as necessary.

- ✔ Distribute meeting details to participants.

- ✔ Gather needed equipment and materials.

- ✔ Determine how you'll use breakout groups.

While you're working out the tactical details of your meeting — like reserving a room large enough to hold the group, getting your hands on the pertinent documents or ensuring the participants clear their calendars to avoid interruptions — give some thought to the meeting's content. The following sections provide more information on setting goals and approaching your meeting with a strategy for success.

Determining the goal of your meeting

A clear goal statement gives purpose and focus to a meeting. More important, it serves as the criterion by which to consider all ideas and solutions. Be a strong facilitator and determine the goal of the first meeting; then assist the team in setting the goal statement for any additional meetings.

Here are some broad suggestions to get you started:

- ✔ Clarify roles and responsibilities within a project or a team.
- ✔ Discuss behaviours that are affecting the team.
- ✔ Change or retool processes that aren't working.
- ✔ Create harmony and renew relationships.

Start with a broad idea of what you'd like to tackle and then get specific before you communicate the goal to attendees. How you state the goal makes a difference in the attendees' attitude and expectations. For example, a goal statement like, 'This meeting is to determine who is responsible for the breakdown in service' results in a group of defensive participants full of accusations and ready to point fingers.

In contrast, 'This meeting is to determine proactive ways to limit the breakdown in services' sets the tone for a positive, productive discussion in which people's ideas and creative thinking are appreciated. Your goal statement should do the same.

Creating an agenda

The agenda serves as a guide for the entire group to follow during the meeting. As people move from large group work to small group work and back again, they can always look to the agenda to know where they are in the process. The best work is often done when time is limited, so keep the meeting moving forward as much as possible. A good agenda includes:

- ✔ Exact start and end times, and break times
- ✔ Participation requirements (including ground rules)
- ✔ Points when the facilitator has the floor
- ✔ Details, details, details

Proposing ground rules

Ground rules allow group members to share information in a respectful manner, creating an environment where ideas are heard and validated. Suggest ground rules that help accomplish the meeting goal, and then give the group the opportunity to create a set of guidelines (or add to an existing set) that everyone can agree to work with. Use them to keep the group on task and to lessen your need to intervene as the meeting progresses. Start with these:

- ✔ Everyone is invited to participate.

- ✔ All ideas are valid.

- ✔ Speak for yourself — avoid 'we' language.

- ✔ Speak respectfully — without monopolising or interrupting.

- ✔ Stay on topic and work to solve the issue.

- ✔ Ask questions instead of making assumptions.

- ✔ Honour each person's right to pass.

- ✔ Follow time limits.

- ✔ Be present by turning off phones and computers.

Display the final ground rules so everyone can see them — they're a good visual reminder of the group's first agreement!

Considering breakout groups

When designing the meeting process, consider making time for small group work. Breakouts can be a welcome change from the large group dynamic and allow people to share more perspectives (they also keep people awake and on point!). For more on the logistics of working with breakout groups, see the section 'Breaking into small groups' later in this chapter.

If emotions are running high and trust is low, consider breaking into small group work right away to avoid the angry mob mentality taking over from the start. If the team conflict hasn't reached a critical point, start as a large group and use small group work later in the meeting.

Adding breakout groups to your meeting plan has many benefits. Breakout groups

- ✔ Give individuals more airtime.

- ✔ Provide a comfortable forum for reticent people to speak.

- ✔ Allow for efficient work on multiple topics or tasks.

- ✔ Provide anonymity and greater safety when issues are difficult or emotional.

> ✔ Furnish a space for problem-solving and proposals that the larger group can refine and approve.
>
> ✔ Deter soapbox speeches from negatively affecting the whole group.

Before you jump in with a plan laden with small group assignments, consider the limitations. Breakout groups

> ✔ Take up valuable meeting time — from deciding how to divide to settling down to reconvening.
>
> ✔ Create more work on your part in the preparation phase.
>
> ✔ May instil resistance in participants who are suspicious of breaking up the larger group.
>
> ✔ May get competitive, leading people to become territorial and go overboard protecting their ideas.
>
> ✔ May make individuals feel that they don't need to participate in the large group work.

Kicking Off the Group Meeting

Because you called the meeting to discuss a conflict, rest assured that everyone will be watching your every move. Employees will scrutinise everything from how the room is set up to how you describe your role. Be prepared, be present and be ready to listen as you facilitate the discussion.

Setting the tone

Welcome all the participants to the team meeting. Be confident and clear, maintain eye contact and don't forget to smile! Your comfort in front of the group will help people relax and will create the open and inviting environment you're aiming for.

Introduce yourself and describe your role as a facilitator. Explain how you'll be assisting the group in the discussions and goals for the day. If you have guests or assistants, introduce them and describe their roles as well.

Read the goal statement for the meeting. Ask for questions and allow time — five minutes at the most — for the participants to understand clearly the task for the day.

Presenting the agenda and finalising the ground rules

Describe the details of what you're asking of the group and the time frame for the meeting. Help the team understand what the large and small group goals are. Remember that your agenda should include time to ask questions and have a short discussion.

Present the ground rules you created beforehand (refer to the earlier section 'Proposing ground rules'), and ask the attendees to add any additional ground rules that are necessary for them to work together (add no more than one or two requests). The entire group must agree (a quick show of hands should do it) to all ground rules before you begin, because you'll use the rules as your moral compass, so to speak, when things get heated or the meeting starts to derail.

Because you can't be everywhere at once, create a version of the guidelines to post at small group stations to remind everyone of how they agreed to participate in this process.

Hearing from the participants

Individuals need to have an opportunity to share their point of view. The goal in a large group setting is to provide this in a way that has structure and isn't a free-for-all. People can share their perspective in the large group or in smaller breakout groups, but take into account how intense the feelings may be and how vocal the group could get. Whatever you choose, consider the following technique.

Provide a framework for people to follow when it's their turn to speak so that they can acknowledge the past but quickly move to the future with solid ideas and a willingness to create something new. Your guidelines for input should include four parts:

✔ **Incident:** Simply describe what happened (the details).

✔ **Impact:** How has the incident affected you personally?

✔ **Change:** What do you feel needs to change?

✔ **Ideas:** What ideas do you have to move forward?

Using intervention strategies

Members of a group often have differing expectations, assumptions and needs. Some members need individual time and attention, and if they don't get it, they may create interruptions. An important part of your job as facilitator is to handle such distractions with appropriate responses so you can move the discussion forward.

Moving around the room can curb disruptions before they occur. Maintaining eye contact with the group — not just the individual speaking — lets others know you care about what they're thinking and feeling.

Your audience needs to feel that participation is balanced and you're an effectual facilitator. So when someone talks out of turn, makes too many jokes or challenges your authority, address the disruption by being clear and assertive and by using a confident tone of voice. Start with low-level, subtle responses, and only ramp up your response when necessary.

Here are some of the more common disruptive behaviours and tips for responding to them:

- ✔ **Challenging the facilitator:** If someone's undermining your agenda, is agitated and confused about what you're doing and why you're in charge, or is making personal attacks, she's challenging you. Interventions are:

  - **Low level:** Remain calm; ask the speaker to repeat the concern for the whole group.

  - **Mid-level:** Validate the concern; ask what the speaker needs to know and what information would be helpful to the group.

  - **High level:** Tell the speaker you'll have a private conversation with her during the break, and then chat with her later to quickly hear her out and ask for her cooperation. Let her know you may have to excuse her from the meeting if the behaviour continues.

- ✔ **Having side conversations:** Side chatter is distracting, disruptive and disrespectful. It also makes people paranoid! Interventions are:

  - **Low level:** Walk over next to the disruptive culprit so he becomes aware the group is focusing on him.

- **Mid-level:** Ask him if he has a question or concern that needs to be addressed, and remind everyone of the ground rules (side conversations are a form of interrupting).

- **High level:** Speak privately with the individual about the disruptions, and ask him for a commitment to change his behaviour.

✔ **Being overly enthusiastic:** Some people may think they have great ideas, talk when they're anxious, or maybe just like to hear the sound of their own voice. Whatever the reason, their over-participation discourages others from engaging in the conversation. Interventions are:

- **Low level:** Thank the individual for her input and ask if anyone else has a point of view to share.

- **Mid-level:** Remind the speaker that you need to follow the timeline in the agenda, and ask her to state the point she feels is the most important.

- **High level:** In private, confront her about the amount of time she's taking to put forth her views at the expense of other people's opinions. Ask her for a commitment to change her behaviour, and offer to provide additional ways she might share her ideas, such as by email or memos.

✔ **Dropping out:** Some people are uncomfortable speaking in public, but if you think a team member isn't sharing for another reason, consider that he may be intimidated by you or others. Or, perhaps he's waiting for a chance to enter the conversation or simply isn't interested. Interventions are:

- **Low level:** Ask for input or questions from those who haven't shared.

- **Mid-level:** Share the importance of each person assessing what he might have to add to the group.

- **High level:** Break into small groups with a specific output expected, or privately ask for the opinion of those who aren't sharing and then ask them to share their response with the group.

✔ **Joking around:** You know the joker types — they're always the first with a witty remark. They may want attention from the group, or they may just use humour to get through tough situations. They often have great ideas if you can break through the silliness. Interventions are:

- **Low level:** Be upfront and clear that you acknowledge the speaker's sense of humour; ask for realistic ideas as well.

- **Mid-level:** Inform the speaker that the humour is getting in the way of hearing other people state what's important to them.

- **High level:** Remind the speaker of the goal for the day and ask her to hold off on the humour until the team completes the goal.

✔ **Exiting:** Yikes! When someone walks out, he's either not interested or highly emotional. Either way, a public exit is a distraction to the group; in fact, distracting the group just may be the motivation behind his grand exit. Interventions are:

- **Low level:** Ask the person if he's willing to stay and share what's happening.

- **Mid-level:** Give the person permission to go. Acknowledge the walkout to the group and allow them to discuss it briefly if they feel the need.

- **High level:** Contact the person after the meeting to discuss the issues.

✔ **Showing a sceptical attitude:** Sceptics are unhappy and troubled no matter what happens, and can sour a meeting without a word. They may have valid reasons to complain, but heckling and using aggressive body language aren't positive ways to handle tough situations. Interventions are:

- **Low level:** Ask the speaker to express her idea or concerns by describing what she'd like to see happen rather than making it clear what she doesn't want.

- **Mid-level:** Ask what it would take for her to believe and trust that things can be different.

- **High level:** Ask her to hold her comments about the past, and explain to her that the group is now focusing on future solutions and ideas. Talk to her privately about the group's need for her support and consider giving her a leadership role in a smaller group.

Breaking into small groups

You can divide any large group into smaller ones in a number of ways: by counting off, using birth month or pulling names out of a hat. However, in a meeting focused on resolving a conflict, do a little strategic thinking and assign people based on your desired outcome.

Hearing from all perspectives in conflict discussions is important, so diversify the groups by job, rank or departments so that different sides are represented. This approach breaks down cliques and creates an even playing field. Individuals who are resistant to discussing the situation may be more willing to consider the opposing point of view if they have the opportunity to discuss it in a small group setting.

Size matters! Use smaller groups for sharing personal information, developing ideas and brainstorming solutions. For example:

- ✔ Groups of two or three are great for more open sharing. They work well when people are new to the team, when emotions are running high or when people feel a need for safety.

- ✔ Groups of four or five are good when you want more energy for defining problems and generating ideas.

- ✔ Groups of six or more are useful for team-building. In a group this size, people have to wait longer before they can speak, creating patience in some and encouraging leadership in others.

Creating specific assignments

Small group work requires focus; a group without focus will be unproductive and could end up creating a new conflict. Be sure that your instructions are clear and concise — everyone should know what your expectations are. Allow for questions in the large group before you break out to smaller groups or you'll spend too much time reiterating your expectations to each small group.

Assigning roles minimises cliques, provides for a freer exchange of views and allows you to place troublemakers or uninterested parties in positions where they must engage in the discussion. Each group needs a scribe to write down ideas, a reporter to convey those ideas to the larger group and a facilitator to manage the conversation.

Keeping groups on task

As the main group facilitator, you're responsible for keeping time for the whole group. Set a time limit for the small group work and ask the groups to be prepared to report back to the large group. Their presentation should focus on highlights of the group discussion, key topics, conclusions and recommendations.

Even knowing the time limit for their work, small groups can have a tendency to focus on the past. Each small group facilitator should be sensitive to the need for people to express their opinions but also be aware of moving the group forward. Give small group leaders permission to use language like, 'I can see how difficult this has been for you. What ideas do you have to resolve the issue?'

Small group work can include prioritising a list generated by the larger group, finding weak spots in current systems, identifying potential snags in suggested solutions or brainstorming on any number of issues. Regardless of the assignment, consider these guidelines:

- ✔ **Provide focus and be clear about your expectations.** For example, if a group is brainstorming, remind the members that they shouldn't also be evaluating or prioritising ideas. Help groups by posting what the task is at each station: 'Remember, your task is to brainstorm ideas only.'

- ✔ **Circulate around the room, answering questions and intervening if flare-ups occur or if groups lose focus.** Be careful to allow people the privacy and confidentiality they need — having a manager overhear the conversation could inhibit them.

- ✔ **Prepare small groups for re-entry to the large group.** Do this by calling an end to the task and giving them five minutes or so to clarify their findings. Give them a break before rejoining the large group to settle any last-minute confusion.

Coming back to the larger group

Each group needs a chance to share new insights and highlights. The process you choose depends on the goal for the meeting and the number of participants in attendance. If the group is large, you need someone to capture and record the ideas shared by the small group reporters.

The goal of coming back together is to get all the ideas in a central location, write them down on a whiteboard or flip chart, and then have the group decide which items are the most important. Follow these steps:

1. **Have each reporter share the ideas from the small groups.**

   It's normal for some ideas to overlap, so clarify whether each idea is truly different from what has already been noted.

2. **Before each reporter sits down, ask group members if they have any additional thoughts.**

3. **After you list all the ideas, lead the large group in an exercise to prioritise the topics.**

   Which ideas do they think are most important to the group's efforts to move forward? I often let everyone share their two cents by giving them two votes that they can place anywhere on the list. This is an efficient way for everyone to have a voice but doesn't drag out voting and campaigning for certain ideas. It also demonstrates, in a very real way, the ownership the group has in the solution.

Devising a Plan for Follow-Up

Summarise the work the team accomplished at the meeting and take some time for the group to celebrate what has been done while you look forward together.

Help the group determine a purpose or goal statement for any future work. This establishes a clear direction, keeping them moving forward with a task, goal and focus in mind. Discuss how the team will keep communication open and what they need for future meetings. Facilitate a discussion on how they'll handle difficulties or unanticipated issues that come up, and how everyone will have access to new information.

Assigning next steps

When you have a focus for the future, assign concrete tasks and actions that meet the team's goal or purpose statement. This action plan is a document that group members can look to when they have questions. Action plans include

- ✔ **What** the tasks are
- ✔ **Who** is responsible for what
- ✔ **When** assignments are due
- ✔ **How** the follow-up will be done

Creating benchmarks

Groups thrive when they can brainstorm ideas, problem-solve, develop alternatives and take action together. By setting benchmarks, the group can easily identify its progress and successes. For example, measuring employee satisfaction and setting a benchmark to increase the current average by two points shows the team that things are getting better when the goal is met. Similarly, if a conflict concerns the glitches in a company process, creating a benchmark to sell more widgets or spend less time filling out forms gives individuals something concrete to work toward.

Report progress to all team members through a newsletter, by email or by reconvening the group. Consistent information assures members that progress is continuing. Finally, subtly assess and observe your team to determine if employees are using new skills or tools to resolve problems, taking personal responsibility for resolving issues on their own, or communicating well during the follow-up time. These are all points of reference that your work is paying off.

Chapter 11

Determining How Your Company Can Help

· ·

· ·

*E*ven if you work in the smallest of companies, you may not be completely on your own when the inevitable conflict arises. Companies that recognise the cost of unresolved conflicts offer resources to help employees resolve issues early on. And those companies that haven't invested in large-scale conflict resolution strategies usually offer at least a few basic services.

This chapter takes a look at the most common conflict resolution resources and helps you determine which option will best meet the needs of your current circumstance. It also looks at how you can help design a conflict resolution system for your organisation — one that addresses current and future dispute resolution goals.

Working with Human Resources

The human resources (HR) department is a valuable resource to anyone in the organisation. Most employees see HR as a compliance office — the place that makes sure everyone is following the rules and regulations. But that's not all HR does. It ensures that your company is implementing policies that protect the organisation, helps managers realise the liability they carry through their actions and sees to it that employees are meeting company expectations. HR receives a complaint, investigates the situation and determines a course of action to protect everyone involved.

HR experts work hard at balancing efforts between employees, the company and the law. Take advantage of their objective viewpoint when you need more information or want coaching on how to handle a problem.

Partnering with you to tailor your approach

In times of conflict, think of your HR department as a partner that can help you create an action plan. HR professionals know what conflicts can cost a company. Although HR staff members definitely have an eye on compliance, they often work beyond documentation to coach an employee through conflict and direct him toward resources that educate and reduce similar situations in the future.

After HR has taken any required steps to document a situation and protect the company, it can also

- ✔ **Provide an employee the opportunity to save face and build confidence.** No-one likes to be reprimanded. Giving an employee the chance to share her perspective and be part of creating a solution helps that person build confidence and feel better about the overall situation.

- ✔ **Provide insights into your management style.** HR can look at how you manage employees and help you identify your strengths and weaknesses — what is or isn't working. They can provide tips on working with staff in a manner that you may never have considered.

- ✔ **Help you manage your employee on an individual level.** No matter how well your management style seems to work for you and most of your staff, you're bound to have an employee who isn't as comfortable with your approach. HR can help you tailor your approach to that individual to reduce conflict and help you get the most out of your employee.

Letting you know when action is required

If you have any concerns that you or your company may be liable because of something you say or do, ask the HR department for help.

HR professionals can advise you when

- ✔ Sexual harassment complaints surface against you or another employee.

- ✔ You're concerned about any act that could be considered discrimination or you've received direct complaints of discrimination.

- ✔ You've received reports that an individual in the company has bullied another person or group of people.

- ✔ There's any indication, threat or act of violence or potential security threats.

If you're unsure whether a scenario should be presented to HR, err on the side of caution.

Providing training resources

HR can be a wealth of knowledge when it comes to providing in-house training or arranging for contracts with outside professionals. Training can be arranged for everything from workplace safety to harassment prevention, and from diversity awareness to conflict resolution skill building.

Accessing employees' work histories

The HR department has probably worked with most employees from the beginning of their careers with the company. They write job descriptions, interview potential candidates and help hire the right person for the job. These people protect the company by keeping detailed records on each employee, so if you're having difficulty with an employee, HR can help by looking into the employee's history to determine if this is a one-time incident or a behaviour pattern.

They should have a record of what strategies have been taken with the employee and can reference previous performance evaluations that include areas that the employee needs to improve, helping you determine your next course of action. For example, if tardiness has only been a problem for an employee recently, a quick chat and schedule adjustment prior to a major disciplinary action makes sense. But if you find that the employee has had many documented warnings about tardiness, a more formal approach with documented objectives and consequences may be the best course of action.

If you ask HR to look into an employee file, be sure to check for any information regarding special accommodations — such as a longer break to receive treatment for a medical condition — that he's legally entitled to.

Identifying employee support programs

Your organisation may offer employee support programs, and these are a great resource if you feel that outside stressors are contributing to workplace conflict. These programs provide a confidential outlet in which to work through many situations that may be out of your control as an employee's manager.

Support programs vary from organisation to organisation, but they usually include free counselling sessions to help staff through a hard time. If an employee needs someone confidential to talk with, check with HR on whether she can be matched with a professional who specialises in a particular area of difficulty, such as:

- ✔ Addiction issues
- ✔ Family care needs
- ✔ Financial counselling
- ✔ Legal referrals
- ✔ Relationship/family dynamics
- ✔ Mental health matters

Investigating mediation programs

No one cookie-cutter standard exists for workplace dispute resolution options, so do a little investigating to see what's available in your company. Options may include mediators or counsellors. All the services may be found in one central location, or you may have to check out different areas and departments for specific resources.

Familiarise yourself with what conflict resolution options your organisation offers, and how people can access these, so you can use the resources and encourage employees to access services on their own. Proactively presenting them to your team as valuable tools that you support encourages their use.

In a typical *mediation program*, the parties involved are assigned a mediator or they can choose a mediator they both agree on. The process is confidential and allows employees the opportunity to return with an agreement that they can share or keep to themselves.

Generally, a mediation program offered by an organisation has trained or certified mediators who can facilitate a discussion between you and another person, or you can refer employees to the service.

Keep in mind that mediation is not a tool to use only when a problem escalates beyond what you can comfortably handle. Use it early on to prevent a problem from getting out of control.

Proactively Designing a Conflict Resolution Plan

Designing a conflict resolution plan means giving several members of the organisation the skills they need to resolve conflicts early, as well as providing a variety of avenues for them to seek support in resolving conflicts. The greater the number of alternatives, the more likely it is your people will be proactive in resolving their own conflicts. Having an array of options available allows people to choose a resource they're most comfortable with and increases the likelihood that they'll resolve conflict before it escalates.

What you can do

You may not be in a position to change the overall culture of your entire company, but you can change the culture of those who work directly for you and share your successes with those up the ladder. If you're not entirely comfortable requesting that the organisation develop a formal conflict resolution plan but want to lead by example, you can consider taking the steps outlined in the following sections.

Offering training

Providing training in conflict resolution helps employees become aware of the behaviours that affect others. It also gives them the skills to begin addressing those behaviours and conflicts on their own. Schedule training that starts with communication basics, demonstrates active listening skills, identifies conflict styles for each person and teaches how to approach a co-worker when conflict arises. Have the team receive the same training (together or at separate courses) so they have a common framework that everyone works from.

Cultivating inside mediators

While usually only possible inside large organisations and the public service, training a select number of employees as mediators can be a great way to supplement the company-wide training. If funds are available for the training, be sure to have a diverse group of mediators so that employees are able to choose someone they're comfortable with. If your work group is small, start with yourself and add others later.

Providing outside mediators and facilitators

Identify resources outside the company that provide conflict resolution services. Having an idea of where you can turn if a conflict escalates beyond your skill set is a smart, proactive move that keeps you from having to scramble in the heat of the moment. Plus, outside mediators or counsellors provide another layer of confidentiality that's an important factor for most employees.

Giving employees multiple ways to access resources

Be sure your employees know everything that's available to them (trained mediators, counsellors, HR, and so on), so they can choose what's most comfortable. If they're limited to contacting only one person for help, they may be less apt to approach conflict from a solutions-oriented perspective.

Make information available in multiple formats and locations so your staff don't have to spend hours searching through employee handbooks to find what they're looking for. The easier it is for employees to access the resource, the more likely it is they'll use it.

Always leaving the door open

No matter how far a conflict escalates, always create an opportunity for parties to come back to the table to resolve it. Even if you're on the verge of a lawsuit, the climate may still be ripe for settling a case. Be open to any requests to settle while you still have some control over the outcome.

What your company can do

Having support from the top down is absolutely necessary for a successful conflict resolution plan to work, so consider who else in the organisation would be interested in adding to and improving your existing resources. If you're currently in the middle of a conflict, now may not be the best time to take on a company-wide initiative, but if you're interested in working with like-minded people to build a system that creates opportunity out of conflict, consider the options covered in the following sections.

Expanding the role of HR

An HR department that's trained in conflict resolution (instead of simply stating policy or documenting issues) could provide added coaching and resources to employees facing difficulties. They can bridge the gap between a company that says it values conflict resolution tools and a company that actually uses resources through a well-written, and actionable, dispute resolution policy. Limiting the role of HR limits the possibilities.

Revising the employee handbook

Employee handbooks typically have a dispute resolution section. If yours only has a few steps before you're required to document behaviours in an employee's file, you're possibly setting up employees to fail right from the start. Emotions that may have been manageable with a different method can spiral out of control when permanent records are involved, so find ways to include steps and language that give employees a chance to make things right.

Choosing a starting point

Be open-minded while you figure out the best way to create a culture that resolves conflict early in your company. Here are some things to consider as you get started:

- ✔ **Determine what conflict is costing the company.** Refer to Chapter 5 for more on this.

- ✔ **Assess what you're doing well and where you can improve.** Refer to the earlier sections 'What you can do' and 'What your company can do' for options.

✔ **Identify key players in your organisation.** Keep sharing resources and include as many people as you can from different areas to build on what exists.

✔ **Research what resources are available in your community.** Most centres are non-profit and use highly trained mediators to resolve a variety of issues, including workplace disputes, at a relatively low cost.

✔ **Start small and track your success.** However you start, track any noticeable changes as a way to show tangible results when you go to bat for more dollars. Keep track of whether

• Employees are having fewer conflicts and managers are dealing with complaints better.

• Fewer complaints are advancing to HR.

• Employee turnover, use of sick leave and tardiness are declining.

✔ **Commit enough money to support your plan for conflict resolution.** Earmarking even a small amount of money each budget cycle to strengthen conflict resolution can provide a solid return on investment.

Chapter 12

Ten Pearls of Wisdom from Professional Mediators

*S*eeing a conflict through to a positive resolution can be life-changing — it certainly has been for me. Helping others, and yourself, through a difficult time is empowering — whether you're at work, at home or at play.

My goal with this chapter is to share what I know about mediation and conflict and to take advantage of the fact that I know some really accomplished and insightful mediators. My hope is that some of this expertise will help you turn problems around in your everyday life without having to become an expert in conflict resolution.

Value the Process as Much as the Outcome

Achieving resolution and securing a signature on an agreement form may be an obvious sign that a conflict conversation has gone well — unless, of course, you steamrolled over the parties and forced them to acquiesce because you wanted to quickly put the surface issues behind you. Striving to improve a working relationship gives you more than a momentary solution. A mediation process that allows the parties to come away with an understanding of the real issues can also deliver broader benefits, such as more collaboration between the two parties, an increase in creativity and a boost in productivity.

Accept That Her Truth Is Her Reality

Acting as the judge, jury and executioner isn't the point of mediating conflict. The purpose of the discussions isn't for you to find out who's telling the truth and who's lying — for the people involved, the stories they share *are* the truth. Work within a person's point of view to help her find resolution.

Rapport Matters

Presenting yourself professionally and being open to input from all sides creates a comfortable environment for both parties to be honest with you about what's happening and what they're willing to do to resolve the difficulty.

Get off to a good start by being genuinely interested in the perspectives of all the people involved in the conflict.

Be Present and Available

Give your full attention to the individuals sitting in front of you during a conversation about conflict — not the computer, not your phone, not the knock on the door. Put the golden rule into play and give others the same care and attention you'd want in the same situation.

Find Common Ground for More Success

People in conflict have a tendency to focus only on differences and these differences are what keep them fighting. Rather than concentrate on what's dividing them, find the things that bring them together. Common interests and values can be the stepping stones to finding solutions that work for both people. Mediators who are able to keep their clients focused on common interests have successful outcomes more times than not, and you can too. Even if a problem is between you and another person, if you can approach the discussion from the viewpoint of the things you have in common, you stand a better chance of the other person relaxing and hearing what you have to say than you do if you only want to discuss your differences.

Be Aware That This Isn't the Participant's Best Moment

People in conflict aren't at their best! Feelings such as hurt, fear, frustration and anger can drive a person to ridiculous behaviour sometimes. That doesn't mean that underneath these feelings a colleague isn't a decent person just trying to get by. Give him the benefit of the doubt, even if you can't see his best qualities at the moment.

Silence Is Golden

Silence is one of my favourite tools! Don't rescue employees when they sit in stony silence. The more uncomfortable they get, the more you demonstrate to them that this is their conflict. If you speak to end the silence, you may take away an opportunity for them to share something important.

The same is true when you're one of the people involved in a conflict, but be careful not to come across as stubborn or defiant. Use your communication skills to ask about the other person's perspective, and then wait for her answers.

Be Curious

Curiosity may have killed the cat, but it's one of a mediator's best tools! My favourite questions start with, 'Help me understand ...' and 'I'm sorry, I'm not quite sure what you meant when you said ...' This gets a person talking so I can listen for what's really important to her — that is, her *values*. (Refer to Chapter 2 for a more in-depth discussion of values.) Priceless!

Fear Rules the World

Giant egos, rude behaviour and bully tactics all come down to the fear of losing something. The bigger the reaction, the bigger the fear. Work to uncover what a co-worker may fear from the conflict and strive to allay his concerns.

Look to the Future

Staying in the past is much like circling the drain; around and around we go. Asking parties to share their perspective (what brought them here) is a good way to start a mediated conversation. Everyone needs a chance to tell her side of the story, but repeating (and repeating and repeating) what happened 19 Tuesdays ago doesn't resolve anything. When you feel the perspective has been heard, move to address it properly by focusing the conversation on what she'd like to see on the next Tuesday, what that looks like for her and how she thinks she could make that happen.

Index

About the Author

Vivian Scott is a Professional Certified Mediator with a private practice in Snohomish, Washington. She has handled a variety of workplace cases, ranging from helping business partners end their relationship with dignity, to creating a new working environment for a law firm. She has completed an extensive practicum and certification program with the Dispute Resolution Center of Snohomish & Island Counties, where she mediates on a regular basis helping parties resolve conflict in workplace, family, consumer and landlord/tenant disputes. Scott is a member of the Washington Mediation Association and spends much of her time advocating for meaningful resolution.

Scott lives with her partner of 11 years, Brent, and is proud mum of a grown daughter, Vanessa, who will soon be a stellar attorney and mediator in her own right. Scott can be reached through her website at www.vivianscottmediation.com.

Author's Acknowledgements

I'd like to thank all the people who played a part in bringing this book to life, including my Wiley friends Mike Lewis, Rhea Siegel, Sarah Faulkner, Elizabeth Rea, Elizabeth Kuball, Todd Lothery and Gary Zimmerman. Big thanks also to the countless family and friends who candidly answered my questions about their personal struggles in the workplace.

The brilliant staff at the Dispute Resolution Center of Snohomish & Island Counties (in Everett, Washington) deserve much credit for their unselfish work and writing prowess. Thanks to the DRC employees for their level heads and warm hearts. Specifically: Ryan Mattfeld, Melissa Mertz, LaDessa Croucher and Kathy Rice.

Special thanks to Gloria Elledge, Kathleen Rostkoski and Anahi Machiavelli for holding down the fort while the rest of us wrote.

Publisher's Acknowledgements

We're proud of this book; please send us your comments through our online registration form located at dummies.custhelp.com.

Some of the people who helped bring this book to market include the following:

Acquisitions, Editorial and Media Development

Project Editor: Charlotte Duff

Editorial Manager: Dani Karvess

Acquisitions Editor: Kerry Laundon

Production

Graphics: diacriTech

Technical Reviewer: Paul Maguire

Proofreader: Jenny Scepanovic

Indexer: Don Jordan, Antipodes Indexing

The author and publisher would like to thank the following copyright holders, organisations and individuals for their permission to reproduce copyright material in this book:

- **Cover Image:** © iStock.com/timsa

Every effort has been made to trace the ownership of copyright material. Information that enables the publisher to rectify any error or omission in subsequent editions is welcome. In such cases, please contact the Legal Services section of John Wiley & Sons Australia, Ltd.

Business & Investing

978-1-118-22280-5
$39.95

978-0-73031-945-0
$19.95

978-0-73031-951-1
$19.95

978-0-73031-065-5
$19.95

978-0-73030-584-2
$24.95

978-1-11864-126-2
$19.95

978-0-73031-949-8
$19.95

978-0-73031-954-2
$19.95

978-0-730-31069-3
$39.95

978-1-118-57255-9
$34.95

978-1-742-16998-9
$45.00

978-1-118-64122-4
$39.95

Order today! Contact your Wiley sales representative.

Available in print and e-book formats.